Early Praise for *Horizons of Joy*...

"When winter arrives in the part of the world where I reside, I often feel an eagerness to embrace the holy darkness and her companions: quiet and stillness. With *Horizons of Joy: Poetic Thresholds for Winter*, I now have a guidebook for reflection. This finely crafted work of creative nonfiction is both contemplative and studious, engaging both the heart and mind. Each offering illumines ordinary—and frequently overlooked—parts of the human experience: horizon, ember, calm, listen, hearth, holly, ornament. This beautiful book both will fascinate those who are curious about etymology and inspire those who are seeking prompts for reflection. This book will be a gift to many!"

> —*Julia Walsh, FSPA, educator, retreat director, author, and host of the Messy Jesus Business podcast and blog.*

Mary Lynne Gasaway Hill, Ph.D., FRSA, is a wife, mother and poet, as well as a professor in the Department of English Literature and Language at St. Mary's University, for which she also serves as the graduate program director. A recipient of numerous teaching and service awards, she is the author of three previous books and a range of scholarly and feature articles. Locally, nationally, and internationally, she has presented research on language, power, and peace and has facilitated retreats and workshops on story, service, and forgiveness. Her course repertoire includes Narrative Theory, featuring an evening of student storytelling, and Writing to Change the World, featuring student outreach on contemporary issues. She has studied in Great Britain, Israel, and Jordan, and has led study abroad trips to London and Northern Ireland. She is the recipient of a United States Institute of Peace grant, the Edward and Linda Speed Peace and Justice Fellowship and is a Fellow of the Royal Society of Arts (RSA). She and her family live in San Antonio, Texas, in the company of the deer, foxes, red tail hawks, caracaras, and Texas barn owls, with whom they share a patch of Earth.

Affiliations:

St. Mary's University, the Royal Society of the Arts, Soul's Journey Poetry Circle, 2e Alamo City, South Central Modern Language Association, Organization for the Study of Communication, Language, and Gender, Corrymeela Peace and Reconciliation Centre, Western Social Science Association, Compassionate San Antonio.

Horizons of Joy:
Poetic Thresholds for Winter

Books by Mary Lynne Gasaway Hill

Horizons of Joy: Poetic Thresholds for Winter

The Language of Protest: Acts of Performance, Identity, and Legitimacy

The Uncompromising Diary of Sallie McNeill, 1858–1867,
co-Editor, with Virginia McNeill Raska

Stories from the Wake:
The Revolutionary Responses of the Sodality of Bordeaux
and Small Christian Communities

Books from:

river lily press

Horizons of Joy: Poetic Thresholds for Winter

Floating Midnight

Flight Patterns

Listening to Light

Midnight Housekeeping

Horizons of Joy:
Poetic Thresholds for Winter

Mary Lynne Gasaway Hill

river lily press

San Antonio   Seattle

Dedication

For Rose Ellen Meyer Gasaway,
whose poems remained private.

For those who did not live to receive a vaccine.
May this book bring some solace to their Beloveds
who now live in the wake of their loss.

Horizons of Joy:
Poetic Thresholds for Winter

©2021 Mary Lynne Gasaway Hill

All rights reserved.

Except for brief excerpts for review purposes, no part of this book may be reproduced or used in any form without written permission from the publisher.

For more information about this book or the author, visit www.horizonsofjoy.com or www.marylynnegasawayhill.com.

ISBN 978-0-9725562-4-8

eISBN 978-0-9725562-5-5

Library of Congress Control Number: 2021918093

First edition 2021

Printed in the United States of America

River Lily Press

Disclaimer: This is a work of creative non-fiction. Unless otherwise indicated, all the names, characters, businesses, places, events and incidents in this book are either the product of the author's imagination or used in a poetic manner. Any resemblance to actual persons, living or dead, or actual events is purely historical.

Cover Illustration inspired by Sister Elizabeth Hatzenbuehler.
Back Cover Photo by Andrew J. Hill, J.D.
Edited by Andrew J. Hill, J.D.
Cover and book interior design by Andrea Leigh Ptak

Table of Contents

Welcome!

elcome to *Horizons of Joy: Poetic Thresholds for Winter*. This collection invites us to take a time out, to enjoy the days shortening and the nights deepening, as we move through our annual cycle of grieving the old and welcoming the new. This is often a time in which we wrestle with meaning, and so this collection also encourages intentionality, in the choosing and using of not only traditionally festive words of the season, but also their common work-a-day counterparts.

For me, raised in the Roman Catholic tradition, Winter has always been shaped by Christmas and the season of *Advent*, from the Latin *ad* meaning *toward* + *venio* meaning *coming*: a movement toward something good, whether that's the birth of the Son in a Christian tradition on December 25th, or the birth of the Sun in more ancient traditions on December 21st. Maybe you celebrate the Twelve Days of Christmas that bridge the old year with the new? Maybe you celebrate Yule or Hanukkah or Kwanzaa this time of year? Maybe you choose not to celebrate any holiday and wonder what all the fuss is about? No matter how we encounter it, Winter is a time when the Earth calls all life to a place of deep rest and contemplation.

Lest we get too literal, this collection is also an invitation to the transformation of Winter that can occur at any time in our lives. Yes, as a planet we experience the season between distinct markings on a well-organized calendar and time-table. However, we know that Winter paints her landscape within us as well. Our personal Winters may last a few seconds or may last much longer than the three to four months of the physical season. Winter is a malleable metaphor for those moments of encounter with starkness, be that a brief meeting in the middle of a day, or a sustained situation that lasts several years.

The following poetic meditations invite us to bask in the cold beauty of the season, as our beloved planet swings on the hinge of the Winter Solstice, closing the door on the old year, to throw open the vistas of the new. These word-paths invite us to wander as we cross that threshold into a new year, a simultaneous linear and circular time: a linear movement from one month and year into the next, a circular movement of the Earth spinning us in the elemental life cycle around the sun. This duality seems appropriate given that the word January finds its origins in the double-faced Roman god *Janus*, who graces entrances and exits. One set of eyes gazes back in remembrance of yesterday; the other set gazes forward in visions of tomorrow. Janus is the god of beginnings, who stands with us and holds our hands, in this in-between space of Winter's threshold.

Thresholds, those sills of doorways, lintels of entrances and exits, are places of liminality, of transition as we move *from-to, in-through, out-of*, a particular place, time or event. In J.R.R. Tolkien's *The Lord of the Rings*, the memorable character of Bilbo Baggins reminds his nephew Frodo that, "It's a dangerous business, Frodo, going out your door. You step onto the road, and if you don't keep your feet, there's no knowing where you might be swept off to." We cross a threshold and we don't know what awaits us. It's a dangerous business, indeed.

Thresholds separate us from before and after, but they simultaneously hold us—even if just for a second—between times, spaces, and events. In this holding, we can be transformed by and through words and deeds, listenings and speakings. As recounted in Krista Tippett's book, *Becoming Wise: An Inquiry into the Mystery and Art of Living*, philosopher poet

John O'Donohue reminds us that the key to thresholds is in how we cross them. Are we crossing in the way he calls *worthily*? If so, we cross with beauty. O'Donohue states, "[B]eauty isn't all about niceness, loveliness. Beauty is about more rounded substantial becoming. And when we cross a new threshold *worthily*, what we do is we heal the patterns of repetition that were in us that had us caught somewhere."

A worthy crossing frees us from the craggy patterns of repetition that our love, kindness, ingenuity, and creativity get snagged upon. How often do we cling to a craggy rock in a dangerous sea because it's familiar, instead of trusting the wind to carry our ragged-cloth-self to a new shore of "a more rounded substantial becoming"?

We know that love plays the long game in the dialectic of our becoming. To paraphrase Hegel, we begin at a starting point; let us call this entrance a *thesis*. We encounter a challenge to that starting point; let us call this holding the *antithesis*. We wrestle with this challenge until we are transformed by it; let us call this exit a *synthesis*. This new synthesis in its time becomes a thesis, itself—until it is challenged by something new, by an invitation to step again on to that lintel to worthily thresh out a new synthesis in love and beauty. Our solstices, Winter and Summer, are just such thresholds, which hold us in our transforming, as the planet rotates through the cosmic dialectic of the seasons. They are global lintels modeling for us a "more rounded substantial becoming" on the planetary scale.

The deep story, or etymology, of the word *solstice* comes from the Latin *sôlstitium: sôl* or sun + the verb *sistĕre, to stand still, to hold in place.* Our Sun, source of light-heat-life, appears to stand still on our horizons twice a year, at the Winter and Summer Solstices, which occur around December 21st and June 21st, respectively. On these days, the Earth and Sun together invite us to stand still on the cosmic threshold, in our paradox of existing in linear and circular time, of being terminally organic in a world where neither energy nor matter can be created or destroyed, of being languaged beings who often find ourselves speechless. Seamus Heaney, in *The Government of the Tongue*, takes us into the paradox of poetry that parallels these Solstice moments, when he reminds us that, "Poetry is more a threshold than a path, one constantly departed from, at which readers and writers undergo, in their different ways, the experience of being at the same time summoned and released." With the gift of such summoning and releasing, how can we not pause, in the embrace of Janus, for a moment or two, to honor Winter's invitation?

The Deep Stories of Words: Horizons, Stillness, Tidings, & Joy

Divided into four themes of *Horizons, Stillness, Tidings,* and *Joy,* this collection summons and releases us to thresh a particular word, such as *wassail* or *twinkling,* by digging into its deep story, reflecting upon it, and then setting that word to work in a poem. Following each poem are prompts, *Pauses at Our Thresholds,* to encourage your own threshing about of the words, ideas or images. Do this in the margins of this book or in its companion journal, or in your own creative space of journal, canvas, clay, song, or other medium. My hope is that the process, of moving from a word's deep story through a poem to a prompt, can serve as a transformative holding space for your own refreshment, whether that takes form as writing, sketching, painting, knitting, or humming an old familiar tune as you wash the dishes. While intentionally ordered for a sustained meditation, each word-path or theme may be engaged in any order by one's self, with a partner, or with a small community. Play gently and enjoy as you wish: A word per day for four weeks? A word per week for twenty-eight weeks? A theme per month for four months? A bit here and there as we bumble along graciously over the course of a year or so? No matter. You choose. Allow yourself the gift of time and spaciousness to rest with these ancient artifacts that we've inherited from our human ancestors: these puffs of air, scratches on paper, pixels on the screen that whisper the Zen prayer of infinite gratitude for what has been, infinite service for what is, and infinite responsibility for what shall be.

This project grew from my own delight and struggle with the Winter season. Each year in our family, the anticipation of Christmas is exquisite. The music. The cards. The decorations and gifts. In our family,

Christmas is a BIG DEAL. But for me, as an individual, the season has always been tinged with grief. I don't ever want to surrender the old year; even though, as Shakespeare's *Julius Caesar* reflects, "death, a necessary end, will come when it will come." And so, the old slips into the new. To cross this threshold worthily, I have to thresh the dialectic of the old thesis into the more rounded becoming synthesis of the new. I have to accept that I cannot rupture time to hold it still. Each year. You'd think that I'd have figured it out by now and gotten over it. However, that's not how it works for me. There's a compound word in Old English, *wintercearig*, that captures this feeling for me. The word combines *winter* and *cearig* or *chary*, meaning *to cause sorrow*. Here it is in the tenth century poem, "The Wanderer," from the *Exeter* Book:

ond ic hean þonan
wod wintercearig ofer waþema gebind,

"and I, abject,
Proceeded thence, *winter-sad*, over the binding of the waves."

Wintercearig. This word, now lost to Modern English, captures my experiences of Winter sorrow, as I struggle with the peculiarity of a liminal time: the week or so between Christmas Eve, my favorite night of the year, pregnant with possibility, gentleness, kindness, and the first few days of the New Year, which too often feel garish and hollow, as another year fades into memory. There is this dying with which to reckon as we jump over the lintel of the old into the new. Perhaps this is why many of my ancestors celebrated the entire Twelve Days of Christmas, from December 26 through January 6? Perhaps they understood, in ways which we, who are divorced from the land and live in grocery-store based cultures cannot, the need for the spaciousness of those twelve days to reckon the *wintercearig*? It is a coming to terms of Winter expiring, *ex spirare*—an exhaling of its spirit, even as this very expiring oxygenates Spring's rejuvenation.

Our Winter seasons are an encounter with this poignancy: Janus simultaneously holds in his hands bitterness, for the loss of the chances and gifts of the past, along with sweetness, for the promise of the chances and gifts of the future. In *Song of Myself*, Walt Whitman asks his readers, "have you reckon'd a thousand acres much?" And, I answer yes—the bittersweet temporal reckoning of the thousand acres of our minds, our thinkings, our feelings, our expectings, our grievings, our fearings, our lovings. We may live in these reckonings for moments or for years, discerning whether it's best to stay with the grief, by letting Janus hold our hands for a while, or to release his hands and rouse ourselves worthily into Spring.

To cross these thresholds worthily, with beauty, we often need kindness and creativity. So, like the ancients before us, we decorate with the tenacious holly and ivy that bare their living to us even in the harshest of frosts. Such decorations clothe the skeletons of our fears and anxieties, of the naked bones of the trees and bushes shivering in the wind, which Winter sketches on her landscape. We swag the garlands, tinsel the trees, and light the lights that befriend the darkness. And we give presents. The giving of gifts can be the vital warm corner in which we let our Beloveds know that they matter; because in the reptilian portion of our biology, we know that the warmth of their presence is a gift. *Present*. What a workhorse of a word—

- of being a gift, an expression of connection. *Thank you for my present.*

- of being aware of oneself and attentively engaged in the moment. *She is present to them in their conversation.*

- of being in a physical location at a particular time. *The child is present in the class.*

Being present and giving presents mark the heavy fluidity of time and our desire to hold it manifest in artifacts of affection. Whether those artifacts are ones of the presence of togetherness or presents wrapped in shiny paper and bows, they are love made visible. It seems fitting then that this generosity of giving also is a key part of Valentine's Day in February, which helps mark our movement toward the ending of the Winter season.

What I am learning through my cycles of *wintercearig* is twofold. First, we have to own ourselves in Winter as fiercely as we do in the other seasons of our lives, so that fear of change doesn't destroy the beauty of it; so that, to borrow from Shakespeare's *Richard III*, the Winter of our discontent can indeed be made glorious summer, not just for a House of York, but for our own Houses, within our own Bodies, within our own Beloved Communities. Second, Winter is not a problem to be solved but an opportunity to delve into, learn about, linger with, and explore that which brings us to a cold stop; it is a transformational invitation to dig deep into that which we cherish. It is a summons to cross the threshold worthily, with beauty, to honor the Great Dialectic of Being Fully Alive, which requires us to reckon the antithesis of death directly.

Aren't we all electrified with living in the moments when we encounter dying? Perhaps this is why we remember where we were when certain dyings occurred: publicly when President John F. Kennedy was assassinated, when the Challenger space shuttle fell from the sky, when the planes were flown into the World Trade Center, Pentagon, and a field in Pennsylvania; or privately when our mothers, fathers, friends and other Beloveds passed over, or when foundational relationships were severed. However, these electrified moments also include the sort of dyings that surface in moments of joy. I have been happily married for over 30 years. But, before I walked down the aisle, as my mother placed a veil on my head, she whispered in mourning, "Does this mean you will always live in Texas?" And we stood very quietly together in a frost of Winter, grieving the loss of our life together as we had known it in Illinois, even as we welcomed our new one. These are all threshold moments of poignancy, bitter sweet moments of Winter Encounter, when all of the stardust in the cosmos is accounted for, rearranged and reconfigured into new forms, shapes, and relationships.

One of the beauties of language is that it provides the means to share this experience of electrified encounter and its transformation of us, from *before* to *after*. The words highlighted in this collection are presents, from and of the human voice over millennia, to support us in our worthy crossings of Winter's thresholds, when we are simultaneously summoned and released from craggy rocks in dangerous seas. I am a linguist by training and am fascinated by the stories that our words carry. We, in turn, carry their stories with us, as we walk out into our daily adventures like Frodo and Bilbo did theirs. This dialectic, between the voices uttering the words and the evolution of the words, themselves, has taken English on a magnificent adventure, horrible and beautiful, as it has evolved as a *lingua franca*, with its words packing tales from long ago and far away. For those interested in learning more about particular words, I encourage diving into the *Oxford English Dictionary*, the source of the etymologies highlighted in this collection.

A Barefoot History

To ground us in this endeavor, here's a barefoot run through the epic tale of English. The language's taproot is a proto-language called Indo-European (IE), assumed to be spoken by those who lived in Eastern Europe and Central Asia sometime after 5000 CE. Over the next few millennia, as IE speakers spread across the land, the language splinters into a dozen or so language families such as Indo-Iranian, Italic, Hellenic, and Germanic. These families give birth to scores of new languages from Hindi to Portuguese to Latin to Gaelic to Farsi and German. They share family resemblances called *cognates*, similar words in different languages. For example, English's *three* has cousins in Latin's *tres*, Greek's *tris*, German's *drei*, Dutch's *drie*, and Sanskrit's *trí*. What we call *English* today is a descendant of Old English of the West Germanic branch. The Angles, Saxons, Jutes, and Frisians brought their West Germanic dialects to Britain, where a Celtic language was spoken, along with the Latin of the earlier conquering Romans. Through alliance, conquest and intermarriage, Old English emerges over the next few centuries; the depth of these new relationships re-christens the island: the land of the Angles, *Angleland*, or England. Over the next millennium, this island is invaded by Vikings, beginning in 793 CE, and then by the Norman French in 1066. These bloody invasions along with subsequent colonization, social life, trade, marriage, and friendship ultimately gives birth to the language two billion people now speak on our planet.

May you enjoy pausing with these words and poems as the sun and moon dance their eternal fandango, moving in harmony, tethered by the unseen.

Horizons

The theme of *Horizons* is drawn from the beautiful story of the word's birth. Originating in Greek ὁρίζων, horizon means *the bounding circle*. We are bound within so many circles, but especially those of each season's horizon. Gazing out on our Winter landscape, we bathe in mirroring silvers, glistening whites, and frosty greys, blanketing Nature's pulse points, nourishing the fallow landscape. It is a time of reckoning, of threshing the wheat and the chaff of our living. What do we wish to take into the new year? What do we wish to leave behind? Do we need to shift our position, posture, or change our gait, when we walk out the door to expand the vision of our horizons? Or is it a time for us to concentrate more intentionally on something closer to home, to contract our horizons? Regardless of where our focus is resting on that internal-external spectrum, our horizons bind us. They bind us even as they beckon us forward, deeper to discovery, challenging us to encounter the dragons, who guard the boundaries of the Great Arc spread before us, that we call home.

Enjoy the words and poems that anchor the meditations rooted in the theme of *Horizons*:

Bright, Mistletoe, Symmetry, Day, Horizon, Night, and *Ember.*

Bright

Pronunciation: 'brIt.   Function: Adjective

Bright has journeyed to us through Middle English, from the Old English *beorht*, akin to Old High German *beraht* bright, and to the Sanskrit verb of *bhrAjate*, meaning "it shines."

Bright, as a well-traveled word of description, represents: *a radiating or reflecting light; a high saturation or brilliance of colors; a high degree of intelligence.*

We begin with this commonly used word, *bright*, as it is one of our oldest ones, spoken by our ancestors thousands of years ago. In Winter time today, we often hear it in several classic holiday carols such as *White Christmas*: "May your days be merry and *bright./*And may all your Christmases be white ..." and *We Three Kings of Orient Are*: "Oh, star of wonder, star of night/Star with royal beauty *bright...*"

While many of us sing this ancient word throughout the holiday season, we also use it to describe the lights sparkling on our trees, the brilliant colors popping off our greeting cards, and our children exploring their intelligence and creativity during this time of profound wonder.

Bright is an adaptable word that vibrates with a sense of hope—hope for us to see more clearly, to gaze more deeply, and to understand more fully the human desire to be *BRIGHT*—luminous, radiant, and brilliant in relation to all of creation. On Winter's horizon, we witness the re-emergence of the *bright* sun as the Earth swings on its Solstice hinge, to bind us in its circle of warmth.

Bright

The sun,
in its wistful winter cloak,
warms
    bright
        the joy of each step
           across the threshold
      between the generosity
of water pure,
of soil rich,
of air fresh,
      and the grace
of a tale told,
of a song sung,
of a hand extended
in friendship,
      as the Earth swings on its hinge
between the
      healing darkness
          and the
      nurturing light.

Pausing at Our Thresholds

1. Consider these dimensions of *bright*—radiating light, saturation of color, and high intelligence—to reflect on all that is *bright* on our magnificent planet, and how hope is derived from the *bright* radiance of our sun. What do you want to *brighten* in your life? What small step might you take to begin that *brightening*?

2. As the Earth swings on its hinge, what tales do you wish to tell in the new year?

3. Step outside. Look to the sky and consider how it animates our idea of *bright*. What is the *brightness* on your horizons these days? What is the darkness? How does their interplay offer you space of healing darkness and nurturing light? Can you draw it? Paint it? Stitch it? Sing it? Dance it?

Mistletoe

Pronunciation: 'mi-s&l-"to   Function: Noun

Mistletoe has its roots in the Middle English *mistilto*, from Old English *misteltAn*, from *mistel*, mistletoe + *tAn* twig; akin to Old High German *zein twig*. It has relatives with Old Icelandic *mistilteinn*, and Danish and Swedish regional *mistelten*.

Mistletoe. As the excuse for sharing a holiday kiss and sparking romance, this well-known *semiparasitic* green bundle, also known as a kissing ball, *has thick leaves, small yellowish flowers, and waxy-white glutinous berries.*

It is a Winter's day. Time to stretch our legs. We wander outside for a walk and look up into the seemingly bare branches of our favorite tree, and there it is: the sacred *mistletoe*, Nature's ornament for her Winter branches.

When we stop to enjoy the splash of green and white amongst the branches, we step into the myths surrounding this plant. This Winter burst of greenery, which lives in symbiosis with its sleeping host, is honored in several traditions.

In Celtic tradition, the ancient Druids hold that all plants and trees have a soul, and that which takes its sustenance from its tree host, holds the soul of the tree. Thus, *mistletoe* wards off evil and is potent for healing, particularly if cut from an oak or apple tree. As part of the Winter Solstice ritual, priests cut down the *mistletoe* using a golden sickle to distribute the sprigs amongst the community.

Italian and Swedish traditions also hold that bunches of oak *mistletoe*, hung in the entryways and ceilings of homes, protect all within from harm, particularly from fire.

In Norse mythology, the goddess Frigga, in an attempt to protect her son, Baldur, god of vegetation, casts a series of spells to make him invulnerable. However, the trickster, Loki, figures out that Frigga had not protected Baldur from *mistletoe*. Loki crafts a dart made of *mistletoe*, convincing Heder, the blind god, to throw it at Baldur in a game. It kills Baldur; but the other gods revive him. Upon his resurrection, Frigga pronounces the plant sacred, declaring that it brings peace to the world, and that all enemies should gather once a year to exchange the kiss of peace.

Mistletoe

The silver sickle
  of a Yuletide Moon
    curves the waning night
      into the expectant dawn.
Its light cascades
  through the bare branches of the oak,
    with its knots of mistletoe –
  shocks of white berries
      nestled within lush green,
tantalizing –
    Just out of reach.

In the tenderness of our Mother's shortest days,
the lips of her wind
brush our cheeks
  with a whisper,
the feather kiss of the holy quiet,
that proffers her promise of renewal.

Pausing at Our Thresholds

1. What *mistletoe* is just out of reach for you on your contemporary horizon? Do you wish to continue reaching for it over the next year? Why? Why not?

2. With whom or with what might you exchange a kiss of peace for the new year?

3. Pause in the protection of one of your thresholds. What is the *mistletoe* that protects you here? Take a moment to honor it, perhaps by intentionally engaging someone or something we are charged to protect: listening to a child or an elder; caring for a pet or creatures in or near our homes; watering and pruning our plants.

Symmetry

Pronunciation: / ˈsɪmɪtri   Function: Noun

Symmetry begins its journey in the land of Homer and Aristotle, with the Greek συμμετρία, parsed as σύν or *sym/sun* as a prefix meaning *with* + μέτρον meaning *measure* or *metre*, plus *-ία*, a suffix that creates a noun, together creating *súmmetros* or *symmetrical.* This well-balanced noun moves westward through Europe, through Middle French *symmetrie*, French *symétrie*, drawing on Italian *simm-* , Spanish *sim-* , or Portuguese *symetria*, or late Latin *symmetria*.

Symmetry. This word captures an essence of *harmony of parts with each other and the whole; fitting, regular, or balanced arrangement and relation of parts or elements; the condition or quality of being well-proportioned or well-balanced.*

Nature offers us the *symmetry* of the horizon, where sand and water stitch the seam of the Earth, where our skylines and streets kiss at sunset, where our known sidles up to our unknown in discovery. With its slide into darkness, Winter demands that we step back to take the long view of the year, recognizing that the harmony between the Winter Solstice and its Summer counterpart is the Earth's metaphor of balance— something we often struggle for in our daily lives. Are we working too much? Are we taking care of ourselves and our family enough? Are we being too competitive when we need to be cooperative? Are we inside when we need to be outside? One of the unexpected gifts of COVID-19 is that it has required a rapid reassessment of our values, forcing us to triage what we cherish and what we can let go of, allowing us perhaps to regain a healthier sense of balance in our daily living. When we focus on a particular spot on the horizon, our vision tends to narrow and its edges blur. If we stay focused on that one spot too long, the proportions of those things we hold dear can slip out of balance. Not from mal intent, but often simply from the sustained effort of having to prioritize one thing over another. The long nights of Winter serve us the warm opportunity to step back, adjust our focus, and regain *symmetry.*

Symmetry

The pale-feathered dove glides in glory
    across an indigo sky,
        lighting on the branch
            that arcs the iridescence

between the Heavens and the Earth.

If God is Love,
then Love is God.
Let us render safe in that symmetry.

Pausing at Our Thresholds

1. What arcs iridescent on your horizons at this time? How does it feed *symmetry* in your life?

2. As you gaze at your horizons, do you notice anything that needs to be adjusted to help move you toward greater balance or harmony? Is there a small change you can make to do this? If so, consider doing it.

3. Pause in the embrace of one of your thresholds. Identify what you might change or accept to render safe in the *symmetry* of Love during this season. Do you have a favorite piece of music where percussion and strings are beautifully balanced? Or, perhaps the music consists of your Beloveds in conversation? Gift yourself time to listen. Maybe invite your Beloveds to listen to the music with you and follow with a conversation about it.

Day

Pronunciation: /deɪ/   Function: Noun

Day appears as an original stone in the foundation of English in its earliest form of *dag*, with cousins in Old Frisian *dei*, Old Dutch *dag*, *dach*, Old Saxon *dag*, Middle Low German *dāg-*, *dach*, Old High German *tag*, *tac*, Old Icelandic *dagr*, Old Swedish *dagher*, Old Danish *dagh*, and Gothic *dags*.

Day is the time *between sunrise and sunset, during which the sun is above the horizon*. More generally, we think of a *day* as the whole period of daylight, including that part of morning and evening twilight when there is sufficient light for life activities. This tiny word, however, is so powerful, that it also means *a period of 24 hours, as reckoned from midnight to midnight, and as the period corresponding to one complete revolution of the earth on its axis*. These three little letters do a lot of work!

We know about *dag*, the earliest Old English form of *day*, from only one source, as a rune name in futhark, the first alphabet in which English was ever written. (It's helpful to think of a rune is to a letter as futhark is to an alphabet). Because we only have this one appearance, the *Oxford English Dictionary* states, that "it is unclear to what extent it [*dag*] should be taken as an authentic form of the English word." That may be a concern for a historical linguist, but not for us. This unique appearance serves as a stunning metaphor for recognizing the distinctiveness, the one-time-only-ness of any of our days, in which we experience the dance of the sun across the horizon, culminating in a kaleidoscope of color that stills us in sunset.

The pronunciation of the word parallels that experience. *Day* starts with that hard stop of breath at our teeth, creating the sound of *d*, but then our mouths open widely to the vowel *ay*, into expansiveness. This also parallels how many of us move through our day, with a harsh jangling into reality with the break from dreaming to waking...and a quest for a good cup of coffee, into an openness to possibility, a receptivity to the dynamism that will engage us as our Earth completes another revolution on its axis, and we are once again blanketed in restful darkness.

Day

How does the Morning leap for thee?
With the least heat of the moon waning and
the brilliance of the new waxing.

How does the Noon time pivot for thee?
With the chime of the fulcrum singing and
the hatch of light opening.

How does the Evening wave for thee?
With the purples and sparkles laughing and
the blessing of the night cooing.

—This poem is a *thank you* to Emily Dickinson as it borrows the initial line from her, albeit in question form.

Pausing at Our Thresholds

1. When we look at the sea from the shore, the part of the sea closest to the horizon is called the *offing*.

What in the offing waves to you with sparkles and blessings for your *day*?

2. What in the offing calls you to pivot toward song and light within your *day*?

3. Think for a moment. Identify what is in the offing that you wish to leap toward during the heat and brilliance of your *day*? Can you create or cook something with words, colors, tastes or smells that can help you make that leap?

Horizon

Pronunciation: /hɒˈrʌɪz(ə)n/   Function: Noun

Horizon, which is one of our four themes, takes a winding path back to its Greek origins, with several Middle English twists and turns, in the forms *orisont, orizont, horizont, orisoun, oryson,* then back to Old French *orizonte, orizon,* and the late Latin *horīzont-em,* and finally returning home in the Greek ὁρίζων, *oryzon, oreezon,* meaning "the bounding circle."

Horizon captures, in its three syllables, our idea of the *boundary of that part of the earth's surface visible from a given point of view; the line at which the earth and sky appear to meet, or the circle bounding that part of the earth's surface visible if no obstructions interfere. It also captures the circle of contact with the earth's surface of a cone whose vertex is at the observer's eye. On the open sea or a great plain these coincide.* These coincide. This co-incidence takes us into the deep wrestlings and compromises of harmony.

We gaze inward, outward and discover the limits of our seeing and understanding for the day; then, we venture a bit further, as the *horizon* binds us, beckoning us forward, deeper, toward discovery. We wonder if there be dragons at the edge of the rings that *horizon* us, their great arcs marking the tango of the sun and moon, encircling all of the living on our Big Blue Marble. If we shift our position, even a wee bit, our vertex adjusts allowing us to experience fresh co-incidences on the open seas and great plains of our lives, in the readings of our hearts, the holdings of our hands, and in the longings of our prayers that shimmer the curve toward tomorrow.

Horizon

In the deep horizon of our heart,
a compulsion to order wrestles
    with the messiness of distraction,
a wonder for wander contends with the warmth of the hearth,
a desire for security threatens the impulse of insight.

In the deep horizon of our heart,
    a firm bed of abundance reclines next to
        a disheveled pantry of lack,
    a tentacle of focus swims next to a sea weed of choice,
    a love untethered speaks next to a fullness of silence.

In the deep horizon of our heart,
        nestled within such plenty,
        we learn ourselves;
            we learn each other,
        roaring, hearkening,
            wrestling, heeding.
        within this bounding circle
            of question and comfort.

—With gratitude to Edward Carpenter's poem "In the Deep Cave of the Heart."

Pausing at Our Thresholds

1. Get up. Go outside. From the vertex of your eye-self, what is the broadest *horizon/s* you are experiencing of your physical world?

2. Sit down. Be still for a moment. From the vertex of your heart-self, what is the deepest *horizon/s* you are experiencing of your internal world?

3. Listen for a moment. What forces are calling for an intense focus on or of your *horizons*? Which ones are calling for a more generous loosening of your *horizons*? What might that intensity, or that loosening, taste like? Can that taste be part of a meal you make today or tomorrow?

Night

Pronunciation: Brit. /nʌɪt/, U.S. /nʌɪt/   Function: Noun

Night, like its partner in rhyme *bright*, has journeyed from the Sanskrit, beginning as *nak*, then through ancient Greek as *νυκτ-*, *νύξ*, then onward to classical Latin *nox*, before picking up Germanic cousins in Old Frisian & Middle Dutch *nacht*, Old Saxon & Old High German *naht*, Old Icelandic *nátt* or *nótt*, Old Swedish & Danish *nat*, and Gothic *nahts*.

Night, despite such wide and varied travels, still means for us what it meant for our ancestral brothers and sisters: *The period of darkness after day. The time at which darkness comes on; the close or end of daylight; nightfall.*

Night fall. Night falls. The falling of *night.* There is a gentleness in the pairing of *night* and *fall.* It comes upon our world with no effort from us, without our permission, slipping quietly over the busyness of our days. The darkness of *night* can swallow our horizons, disorienting us as the grounding clarity of day recedes, setting loose the fairies, pixies, demons, and banshees that sunlight often holds at bay, but moonlight sets free. These fairy tale companions dance through our *nightfall* dreams often, simultaneously kicking up fears and anxieties, as well as courage and aspirations of what could be. *Night* during Winter pulses with possibility, allowing us time to lick our wounds, let healing unfold, and assess the damage done in the bright sun of the day. At this time of year, *the time at which darkness comes on* cloaks us in its Winter robes for many hours more than its counterpart day, granting us a spell of respite, of dreams and imaginings in which we might allow ourselves to wander and wonder.

Night

Our night is silent,
pregnant with the promise
of a Love gone rogue,
a love bursting boundaries,
and the stories of old.

A love that commands a steadfast resistance.
A love that demands a gentle persistence:
>to turn the other cheek,
>to listen to the child speak,
>to feed the hungry
>>and the poor,
>to soothe the agony
>>of too-often war.

A Love gone rogue,
seeding the plight,
of wonder being born
on a silent night.

Pausing at Our Thresholds

1. What are you seeding in these silent *nights* on your Winter horizons? What is the promise of Winter for you? For your loved ones?

2. When you wake in the middle of a Winter's *night*, how does love envelop you?

3. Take a moment right now. Consider how Love has gone rogue in your life by not obeying the rules you've made or society has made. How can you harness that rogue energy, to traverse new horizons in the Spring?

Ember

Pronunciation: Brit. /ˈɛmbə/, U.S. /ˈɛmbər/   Function: Noun

Ember is an ancient word from the Old English *ymbren*, perhaps a corruption of Old English *ymbryne*, meaning *a period, revolution of time*, with *ymb/ about, round* + *ryne/ course, running*.

Ember moves through and out of our mouths almost like a sigh, starting in the back with an *e* and then to the front with an *r*. *A small piece of live coal or wood in a half-extinguished fire*. We use this word chiefly in the plural as *embers*, or *the smouldering ashes of a fire*.

Whereas *ember*, as bits of smoldering ashes, is believed to have come to us through the Old English meaning *a revolution of time*, it's also possible that this dusty word has roots deep in religious ground. There is a custom within Christian traditions of observing Ember Days, which is a cluster of three days (Wednesday, Friday, Saturday), designated four times a year, to mark the beginning of each season. J. M. Neale in his *Essays of Liturgiology* (1863) muses that:

"The Latin name has remained in modern languages, though the contrary is sometimes affirmed, *Quatuor Tempora*, the Four Times. In French and Italian the term is the same; in Spanish and Portuguese they are simply *Temporas*. The German converts them into *Quatember*, and thence, by the easy corruption of dropping the first syllable...we get the English *Ember*. Thus, there is no occasion to seek after an etymology in embers ..."

Traditionally, these *Ember* Days are ones of fasting and prayer to welcome the coming season and give thanks for the passage of the receding one. *The Old Farmer's Almanac* states that the seasonal dates and themes are:

Spring: the Wednesday, Friday, and Saturday after Ash Wednesday, to give thanks for the rebirth of nature and for the gift of light (usually flowers are offered at this time);

Summer: Wednesday, Friday, and Saturday after Pentecost, to give thanks for the wheat crop;

Fall: the Wednesday, Friday, and Saturday after the Feast of the Holy Cross (September 14), to give thanks for the grape harvest; and

Winter: the Wednesday, Friday, and Saturday after the Feast of St. Lucy (December 13), during the third week of Advent, to give thanks for the olive crop.

As we close the theme of Horizons, the history of *ember* reminds us of the devotion of the sun's fire, of its smoldering ashes that light our creativity in the darkness of Winter, that warms our compassion in response to the suffering in the world.

Embers

Ripples of your steps
    fold into the ripples of mine.
An exchange of atoms,
    of molecules,
        of unseen forces,
we move in different directions –
    before ebbing and flowing
back together again.

In our ancestral garden,
Energy can neither be created nor destroyed;
Matter can neither be created nor destroyed;
but Meaning can be –
Love can be –
if their malleability
              is frozen by incessant action,
denied the deep work of winter respite,
    in the jeweled caverns of our being.

Such rest thaws the icy ashes,
makes ready the hands
of Meaning and Love to claw out from within,
gather the embers,
and fertilize the furrows
    of impending choice.

Such nourishment begets the splendor
of the sun re-incarnate,
as its searings stand sentinel
for the sacred turning,
of our phoenix rise,
from the cinders
    of our burning days.

Pausing at Our Thresholds

1. What are the *embers* that are warming you this season? How do they light your Winter horizons?

2. What are the *embers* that are scorching you that need to be squelched? How do they singe your Winter horizons?

3. Stop and rest. Can you take the next ten minutes, or maybe even the rest of the day, to fertilize the furrows of the choices to be made in the upcoming year? If possible, spend this time with a candle burning or near a fire.

Stillness

The theme of *Stillness* arises from its West Germanic tale of *silence, tranquility*, and of its now obsolete meaning of *secrecy*. Winter invites us into its *freedom from disturbance, distraction or agitation*, so we may become free in its tranquility. To become still. After the ebullience of Summer, and the fashion show of Autumn, Winter descends upon us, wrapping us in blankets of basic need: warmth against the cold, shelter from the wind, light out of darkness. We shove our chapped hands into deep pockets for warmth, stomp our feet to get our blood flowing at the bus stop, and run across the parking lot toward a door rimmed with a yellow glow, splashing out on the argent landscape of evening. We are moving into the night depths of the year. The other animals, with whom we share our planet, know that this is the time to hibernate, to slow, to renew and rejuvenate. They know that the momentum that bursts forth into Spring is only possible through this season of *stillness*, a reckoning time, inviting us into conversations and connections with the multidimensionality of our living.

Enjoy the words and poems that anchor the meditations rooted in the theme of *Stillness*:

Yearning, Calm, Believe, Listen, Stillness, Imagine, and *Snow.*

Yearning

Pronunciation: Brit. /ˈjəːnɪŋ/, U.S. /ˈjərnɪŋ/
Function: Noun and Verb

Yearning, like *ember*, has its roots in the earliest recordings of the English language. Through its history, the form of *yearn* has evolved from the Old English *gyrmeð* and *girnan* to Middle English *ʒarne* and *ʒeorne*, amongst many other forms. It has cousins in Old Saxon *girnian*, Old Icelandic *girna*, and Old Swedish *girna*.

 Yearning tingles with change and the possibility of transformation. It *relates to desire or longing, or the expression of this. To have a strong desire or longing for; to crave, covet. Now archaic and poetic.* The evolution of its very form, from Old English *gyrmeð* and *girnan* to today's *yearning*, models change for us, as we transform to meet the *yearnings* of our own lives.

 It's sort of a strange thing, isn't it, to have an action that takes place within ourselves, and not without—even though it may be directed toward something external? We *yearn* for *something*. It is a verb that always requires what grammarians call a direct object, that which receives the action of the verb. We desire something; that something is the direct object. Maybe it is something abstract like happiness or peace? Maybe it is something concrete like a home or a new job? Maybe we long for something fresh in the future, or something that has been lost to the past? No matter. It is certainly an action that can pull us out of the present. If we're not careful, we can miss recognizing the fulfillment of our *yearnings* when they are right in front of us. Taking time to be still offers the opportunity for such recognitions.

 Yearning is also a verb that generally requires a preposition to follow it. Do you remember that part of speech called prepositions? They are those short relational words like *about, over, for* or *after* sprinkled through our daily conversations. Prepositions are bridges, they connect one thing with another, like *yearning* and a partner, or *yearning* and happiness. We *yearn* **for** love, freedom, a bit of stillness. We *yearn* to run **for** office, apply for a more challenging position at work or step back **from** work, focus **on** our loved ones, learn **about** gardening, visit **with** an old friend.

When we are still, we have a chance to let our *yearnings* percolate to the surface of our thinking, prod us a bit, maybe even move us toward scratching the itch of that desire. Often, risk is the play date of *yearning* and so we avoid looking it straight in the eye. But, perhaps this Winter, we can welcome the *yearning*, cherish it in stillness, and imagine satiating that longing that sets us in a prepositional relationship to or with someone or something. What portraits might we paint when our deepest longings are handed a brush?

Yearning

A poinsettia,
the sunflower of winter,
    reddens in the corner,
        next to the fireplace.
Its blush yearns for the short night,
    when the animals talk with each other,
    and "children,
    from one to ninety-two,"
dream of lights glowing
in the warmth of a home,
snow-dusted with love.

—Do you recognize the phrase "children from one to ninety-two"? If so, it's probably because you hear it or sing it in December. It's from "The Christmas Song," which was written in 1945 by Mel Torme and Robert Wells.

Pausing at Our Thresholds

1. For what are you *yearning* during this Winter season? Is there anything preventing you from feeding this desire? If so, might a few moments of stillness help you flow around the obstacles?

2. For what is it that your loved ones are *yearning*? Might yours and theirs dovetail so that you might support each other?

3. Give yourself a couple of minutes to be still. How might your *yearnings* feed your poinsettia-self, allowing your leaves to transform from a rich green to a radiant red? What is an image of *yearning* that you carry in your heart-mind or physically in your pocket as a talisman or tangible reminder?

Calm

Pronunciation: Brit. /kɑːm/, U.S. /kɑ(l)m/, käm, kälm, ko(l)m, New England also 'k[a']m
Function: Noun and Verb

Calm was birthed from the Greek *kauma*, from *kaiein*, meaning *to burn*. It then ignited in Late Latin as *cauma* or *heat*, then in Old Italian *calma*, and finally, spread into Middle French and Middle English, *calme*.

Calm offers simultaneously a sense of expansiveness, when we define it as *a period or condition of freedom from storms, high winds, or rough activity of water or a state of tranquillity*, as well as a sense of containment, when we define it with its secondary, not nearly as well-known, meaning of a *mould in which metal objects are cast*. This dual nature prompts a consideration of how we might cultivate *calm*, a state of tranquility, as a mould for our lives; how we might cast ourselves within a *mould of calm*. As a verb, *calm* can be used literally or figuratively: to *calm the sea or wind*; to *still, tranquillize, appease, pacify*. It can also be used in the form of *becalm*—as a delaying or stopping of a ship at sea by a *calm*.

Calm's story originates as heat, as in *heat of the day* in Greek. Eventually, it unfolds as taking a *rest in the heat of the day* in Romansh and Provençal, and to our contemporary sense of *tranquility*—as well as a *mould into which to pour molten metal* to set and take shape as something newly created. We tend to think of *calm* today as a state of tranquility. But what if we stepped back and unpacked this tale to activate its ancient wisdom? What if we recognized *calm* as a source of heat, as a burning within us, around us, even on the high seas on which we may find ourselves adrift? What if we really could pour ourselves into a mould of *calm* to let it shape us into something new? What might that feel like?

The following poem offers an experience of how actually saying the word *calm* feels. This word takes us from its opening sound of what we called a 'hard c' when we learned phonics in grade school, through the movement of air of a soothing, rich, low vowel, followed by the liquid movement of our tongue folding up, and then the air stopping at our closed, quieted lips. The movement of the word through our mouths helps us sense its meaning; tracking the physicality of saying the individual sounds of the word *calms* us. I don't think it's a coincidence that *calm* is a near rhyme with om, considered the most sacred mantra in Hinduism and Tibetan Buddhism, appearing at the beginning and end of most Sanskrit recitations, prayers, and texts. Such attentiveness to the corporality of our speaking can help to move us to a place of stillness.

Calm /kɑ(l)m/

/k/ It begins with the cracking open sound
             of an egg revealing its gold,

/ɑ/ then slips into the richness of a full vowel,
                         luxuriant of breath,
                              open

/(l)/ that languidly melds with the liquid,
                           closing

/m/ and slides into the mmmmmm of a delicious completion of the circle.

                    A still point of grace
                    in our daily living.

Pausing at Our Thresholds

1. How might *calm*, a still point of grace in the day, mould your anxieties?

2. How do you conjure or imagine *calm*? What does it look like for you to be *becalmed*?

3. Rest for a moment. What yearnings are burning within you that need to be kindled into *calm*, so that its heat might warm you in this season of reflection? What might the touch of that warming feel like? A favorite blanket wrapped around you? A favorite pair of socks knit by an old friend?

Believe

Pronunciation: Brit. /bɪˈliːv/, U.S. /bəˈliv/, /biˈliv/
Function: Verb

Believe possesses a genealogy that is—almost—beyond belief. The tracks of this modern English word lead us to an Indo-European root **leubh*, which is the same root for *love*, which grew into a Proto-Germanic verb **galaubjan*, meaning to *esteem, hold dear, to trust* (the * next to the word means that it's a historical reconstruction based on different forms of the word from across different times and places).

    Believe, Love, Esteem, and *Trust* attend the same family reunions, distinct now, but still bearing a resemblance to one another. *Believe* carries the meaning of *confidence or faith in, and consequently to rely on or trust in, a person, principle, institution, practice or a god.* It involves an *acceptance of the truth and accuracy* of that which we *believe* in. In the 18th century, it also carried the sense of authenticity with it, an assumption that we *believed* in that which we found authentic.

    What an amazing family! But are we really surprised? Just as our individual bodies require the structural elements of oxygen, hydrogen, carbon, and nitrogen, our social body requires the structural elements of *belief*, love, trust, and esteem. Aristotle pointed out to us, several millennia ago, that we are social animals. Social animals who risk *believing*, loving, trusting, and esteeming one another through the Winters of our discontent and the Summers of our satisfaction. These verbal works of art stand in for what's most fulfilling about being in relationship with each other, with our natural world, and with our own sense of purpose. As the nights grow longer, to *believe* has been critical to human survival, from the times when our ancestors gathered together to pray for the return of the sun as the Earth swung on the hinge of the Winter Solstice, to our contemporary moment in which we grasp the scientific precision of the rotation of our generous planet around our munificent star. *Belief* remains elemental during Winter manifesting itself in delightful ways: in a child in a manger; in the lights of Hanukkah; in the drums of Kwanzaa;

in the spontaneous generosity from expected and unexpected sources; and in the existential questions of purpose that surface when we accept the Earth's annual chilly invitation to stillness. *Believe* in the grace born of such stillness, for it is grand.

Believe

Love's Kinsman is **Belief.**
First cousins born,
of a Solitary Word
⠀⠀⠀on an ancient hearth,
genetically linked,
through linguistic alchemy,
with **Trust** and **Esteem.**

This Quartet hums in harmony,
forged into the Stable Molecule
⠀⠀⠀from which the fruits of the Earth arise,
by the tides of long ago winds.

Love + Trust + Esteem + Belief
gambol
in the frosty magic
⠀⠀⠀that blankets the fields in respite,
⠀⠀⠀⠀⠀⠀after the flurry of plow, seed, and harvest;
in the running of the violin's strings
⠀⠀⠀that jettisons our souls skyward,
⠀⠀⠀⠀⠀⠀bathed in joy;
in the holding of the hands of musician and farmer,
while their steps keep time,
⠀⠀⠀with the rhythm of the sleeping field.

Love + Trust + Esteem + Belief:
⠀⠀⠀the melody of the Cosmic Waltz,
⠀⠀⠀⠀⠀⠀where Sun bows to Moon,
⠀⠀⠀to honor the symmetry
⠀⠀⠀of the seasons.

Pausing at Our Thresholds

1. What do you *believe* in?

2. How do love, trust, esteem, and *belief* manifest in your day? Do they resonate in harmony or are they discordant? Why?

3. Pick up a pen. Grab a piece of paper. Write down the names of someone/something that you love, that you trust, that you esteem, that you *believe* in. How do you exhibit or manifest these feelings? Would the people closest to you be surprised by whom or what you have named? Make a collage of this quartet from pictures or other artifacts and invite someone else to do the same. Then share them with each other in a Winter visit with a good cup of coffee or tea.

Listen

Pronuniation: /ˈlɪs(ə)n/   Function: Verb

Listen journeyed across the English Channel, sometime in the middle of the first millennium BCE, as the Old Germanic **hlusinôjan*, with the first Anglo-Saxon invaders of the British Isles. In Northumbria, it took the form of *lysna*, evolving into Middle English *lustnie*, *lustin*. The forms of *listen* with the letter *t* as part of their spelling result from an association with the synonymous *list*, a form still heard today when Shakespeare's most famous ghost pleads to be heard by his son in the opening of *Hamlet*: "List, Hamlet, list."

It seems appropriate that *listen*, as we know it, evolves from a conversation between Old Northumbrian *lysna* and Old English *hlosnian*, both descendants of that Germanic ancestor **hlus-*, meaning *list*, as in *to give ear to, to hear attentively, to pay attention to, to make an effort to hear something*.

Listen. A rather countercultural activity as we scurry to get our point across to our colleagues, bosses, friends, families, in our desire to be heard ourselves. Like stillness, *listen* has been steadfast in the language surviving the Vikings and the Normans, *to give ear* to the radical transformation of the Old English world and its words. Its survival models adaptation for us today as our world is transformed by needed social movements, not-needed pandemics, and an Earth that can no longer tolerate the polluting misbehavior of her children.

Respect for one's self and for others is inherent in deep *listening*. Dean Jackson says, "Listening is an art that requires attention over talent, spirit over ego, others over self." Yes—and sort of no. To *listen* fully to others, we must learn to also *listen* to ourselves, to our deepest yearnings that visit us as ghosts in the night, revealing to us the desires hidden in the attics of our hearts. Such listening can fuel healing and growth with its warmth during this season of rest. It is a restoration of ourselves, when we give ear to our own yearnings, which then allows us to be fully present when we listen to others.

Listen and silent—same letters, simply rearranged. Paul Tillich reminds us that "The first duty of love is to listen." Knowing what we do about the history of the word *love*, I'd expand that to include not just love, but belief, trust, and esteem as well. Trusting in Winter's rejuvenation beckons us to *listen*—and to *listen* compassionately. Compassion comes from the Latin *com-/with* plus *pati/*to *suffer with*. To be compassionate, we are intentional. In our stillness, we witness the dialectic between risk and hope, suffering and joy, shadow and promise. When we *listen* compassionately, we open ourselves to the benevolent power latent in the stories of so many of our fellow voyagers.

Listen

Pause in a moment of solitude –
    at your desk
    in the broom closet
    at your kitchen sink
    in the car –
before you write the email,
sweep the floor,
wash the dishes,
turn the key –
Observe your hands.
Rub the palms together so fast that the sparks of heat
tingle the flesh to the bones
from thumb to pinkie.
Rest the electrified flesh and bone on your chest.
Listen to the hum of your life force:
the frequency of sound waves
of heart in melody with hand.

Pausing at Our Thresholds

1. As we sit with our Winter yearnings, we *listen*. Where is our attention? Are we *listening* with compassion?

2. In Shakespeare's most famous play of the same name, Hamlet's father, the late king, pleads with his son, "List, oh list, Hamlet ..." (1.5.22). What memories or ghosts are imploring us to *listen* this Winter? What tales do we need to *listen* to on the midnight breeze?

3. Place your hands on your chest. Feel the ebb and flow of your personal tides. How do you practice self-compassion, in tune with the hum of your own life force, when you *listen* to others?

Stillness

Pronunciation:/ˈstɪlnɪs/ Function: Noun

Stillness is created by marrying the adjective *still* to the suffix *-ness*. It's cousins with the Old High German *stilnissi*, and has a multitude of Germanic ancestors, such as Old English *stille*, Old Frisian *stille*, Old Saxon *stilli*, and Middle Dutch *stille*.

Stillness in the bleak midwinter, to borrow Christina Rossetti's poignant phrase, edges us, horizons us, nurtures us to an *absence of movement or physical disturbance; Freedom from tumult, strife, agitation, or self-assertion; tranquillity. Silence.* Deep in its history, *stillness* also carried a meaning of *secrecy*, although that sense has grown obsolete, according to the *Oxford English Dictionary*. However, perhaps that sense really isn't obsolete—as so often, when we risk cultivating *stillness*, we discover secrets deep in the marrow of our being.

As a word, *stillness* is steadfast. Why? It survived the onslaught of the Vikings in the late eighth century and then that of William the Conqueror and the Normans in 1066—invasions which flooded Old English with new words and grammar, transforming it from the tongue of the *Beowulf* poet to that of Chaucer, and eventually that of Shakespeare, and beyond. *Stillness.* Its simplicity is beguiling. How many times do we say to a fidgety child, *"just be still,"* even though we ourselves struggle to be *free from agitation or self-assertion*, even though we ourselves often fear *tranquility or silence*? *Stillness* is countercultural: How can we be earning more or doing more if we are just being in *stillness*? *Stillness.* The bleak midwinter calls us to this *freedom from movement and tumult*, calls us to be quiet enough that we can delve into the *secrecy* of the darkness, that cradles the rebirth of the light into the glory of Spring.

Stillness

In the midst
of the ting tang chime of notifications
slides the sing sang rhyme
of stillness.

It feathers the brick and mortar
    of our days,
easing through the cracks
    with jewel-toned rays,
from a window suddenly opened.

The wren,
    prophet of the morning star,
quiets her breathing,
    nestles into awareness.

Awake to aria and requiem,
She sings her praise of welcome.

Pausing at Our Thresholds

1. What are you welcoming into *stillness* on this day? Why?

2. In the Winter hush of *stillness*, what secret dreams nestle in your marrow, readying to take flight in Spring?

3. Quiet your breathing. Even as the world rushes to tweet, text, and respond to the notifications from all of our electronic devices, what are the jewel-toned rays feathering this moment for you? What colors are they? Do you have some crayons or colored pencils to sketch out the rays? If not, do you have any colored paper or magazine pages or advertisements from the mail that you might cut into jewel-toned rays to tape or paste into a journal or on a poster board?

Imagine

Pronunciation: Brit. /ɪˈmadʒɪn/, /ɪˈmadʒn/, U.S. /ˈmædʒ(ə)n/
Function: Verb

Imagine arrives with the Norman conquerors of the island of Britain sometime in the twelfth century as *imagener, ymagener,* or *ymagyner.* Before crossing the English Channel, it roamed from its Latin home of *imāgināre* through the fields of Catalan, Spanish, and Portuguese *imaginar,* to the Italian *immaginare.*

    Imagine sparks our creativity to *conceive in the mind as a thing to be performed; to devise, plot, plan; to represent to oneself in imagination; to form a mental image of, picture to oneself something not real or not present to the senses.* *Imagine* bucks off tradition, unleashes the fecundity of our minds to greet challenges and possibilities—to bring to fruition or to let lie quiet in stillness.

    Imagine, John Lennon's famous song, christens encouragement in our minds to run free across the fields of human experience, to light sparks of possibility, for moves toward love and peace, toward compassion, thoughtfulness, and forgiveness. The stillness of Winter offers us the longitude and latitude of those fields to be explored in the deep nights in which we rest, knowing the Earth rotates on her axis and that the sun will return. The still point of the Solstice, that hinge of renewal swinging open, models for us a rakish, jaunty dare to do the same: to form a picture in our minds of something not yet present externally, but alive and opening within us internally, such as a rejoiced world that dances with the delight of our gifts shared.

Imagine

Imagine the fluttering of so many wings of compassion
that the tides swell in generosity,
shattering the calculus of possession.

Imagine the fluttering of so many wings of thoughtfulness
that the pages of our richest books burst open,
unleashing their wisdom to the winds.

Imagine the fluttering of so many wings of forgiveness
that the ground trembles with the voices of all creatures,
proclaiming:
Peace on Earth. Good Will to All.

Pausing at Our Thresholds

1. In the stillness of Winter, what forms take shape in your mind with the fluttering of your own wings?

3. What are the sorts of wings with which you want to fly when the snows melt and the world cracks open into the new year?

4. Close your eyes. Still your breathing. What *imaginings* in your mind's eye bring joy? Can you say it out loud? Even if just in a whisper? Can you risk writing it or sharing it with a friend?

Snow

Pronunciation: Brit. /snəʊ/, U.S. /snoʊ/
Function: Noun and Verb

Snow, from Middle English *snawe*, has a large Germanic family: the Old English *snAw* or Old Frisian **snê*; Old High German *snEo*; Middle Dutch *sneeu*; Old Saxon *snêu, snêw-*, and Old Norse *snǽr, snjár, snjór*. It also has many cousins in cognate languages: Lithuanian *snëgas*, Old Church Slavonic *snegŭ*, Old Irish *snechta*, Latin *nivis*, and Greek *νίφα, nipha*.

Snow tumbles from the heavens as *precipitation in the form of small white ice crystals formed directly from the water vapor of the air at a temperature of less than 32°F (0°C)*, or as *a descent or shower of snow crystals*; As it blankets the Earth, snow also *conceals or covers, shuts in, or imprisons with*, which leads to a rather different definition: *to deceive, persuade, or charm glibly.*

The hush of *snowfall*. It quiets our world. Meteorologists tell us that as *snow* falls, it is porous and acts like the sound proofing in our buildings, absorbing sound waves, muffling their edges and volume. But, when *snow* melts and re-freezes, it hardens and reflects the sound waves, sending them skittering across its icy surface. *Snow*'s adaptation to its environment models for us a healthy way to go with the flow as our lives change. *Snow*, when it is porous, is open and accepting of cacophony and music, chatter and conversation, equally. But when it refreezes, it lets harm slide off and away, protecting the tender ground beneath its icy shield. It takes it all in, sorting the waves quietly, discretely, covering some, while concealing others.

"A fall of *snow*." This phrase was once used regularly, but now it is rare. When the *snow* is pleasant, we say *snow fall*; when it is frightening and dangerous, we say *snow storm*. It is all part of the water cycle in its seasonal waltz with the weather cycle. So, too, as in our living cycle. Sometimes, in the stillness of our Winter, we need to be porous, open to what is falling about us, allowing it to cover us. But, not all of the time. Sometimes, we need to melt, get slushy and messy, maybe even be inconvenient for someone else. If necessary, we may need to reassess and re-freeze in order to reflect and deflect harmful sounds, those that do not nurture restoration or travel with love.

Snow

Snowing
softly,
the sapphire velvet loosens
its nightly braid,
lets tumble the rosy ribbons of dawn,
just
      as the turning
           sets the world afire.

Pausing at Our Thresholds

1. What do you hope to absorb, like fresh *snow*, in the stillness of this Winter?

2. What do you hope to deflect or reflect, like an ice shield, in the stillness of this Winter?

3. Take five minutes to think about this in the morning. Arrange the day to support these hopes. Can you close your eyes and imagine these hopes playing out in your day? Can you trouble shoot any obstacles that may block your hopes today?

Tidings

The word *Tidings* is shared with us through the generosity of Old Scandinavian. As our third theme, it conjures the excitement and warmth of meeting up with an old friend to exchange greetings or information of importance, as the days shorten with the promise of lengthening. There is a formality, a dressed-up feeling to *tidings*, a word for a special moment of import and impact, that has evolved over generations, as opposed to its workaday counterpart of *news*. There is a sense that when we utter the word *tidings*, it taps into a long-faded time when a herald or town-crier would deliver *Tidings of Good Will* in the village square, or when the majesty of the mountains would declare them, as John Muir reminds us, in *The Mountains of California*: "Climb the mountain and get their good tidings." *Tidings*, like their cousin *tides*, have an ebb and flow to them. We have a moment before they lap at our ears, and then after they fade into effervescence. On the threshold of their hearing, we stand transformed by their touch.

Enjoy the words and poems that anchor the meditations rooted in the theme of *Tidings*:

> *Hearth, Tidings, Be, Holly, Ivy, Auld Lang Syne*, and *Dance*.

Hearth

Pronunciation: Brit. /hɑːθ/, U.S. /hɑrθ/   Function: Noun

Hearth hails from the Germanic family and is cognate with Old Frisian *herth, principal residence of a family,* Middle Dutch *hert, haert,* family inheritance, home, Old Saxon *herth, hearth,* Old High German *herd,* which is probably an association with *erda* earth, floor, ground. Further etymology is uncertain, but perhaps it may be an extended form of the same Indo-European base as Old Icelandic *hyrr* fire and Gothic *hauri* coal, although connections outside Germanic are very uncertain.

Hearth is often where our heart is: *the part of the floor of a room where a domestic fire is made, typically below a chimney against a wall and often the focus in the room; the floor beneath the grate of a fire; the area, often paved or tiled, in front of a fireplace.* The heart of our home.

A hearth can be a private place for tidings. In the fourteenth century Middle English poem, *Cursor Mundi* (The Runner of the World), the poet offers us one of the first uses of the word tidings:

Þe maydyn ranne hame tiþandus to tel/
the maiden ran home tidings to tell.

In our imaginations, we can see this maiden running through the village streets of a medieval Northumbrian town, anxious to share her tidings with her loved ones at the family hearth. It is easy to imagine, because we have done the same, racing home to the center of our lives, whether that's to the kitchen where our loved ones are making dinner, or to a plateau in the mountains, or around the corner to our favorite coffee shop. These *hearths* cradle us in the compassion and mystery of daily tidings.

The maiden ran home to tell her tidings to her loved ones. Her *hearth* awaited her in her home, the seat of communion with her family. Perhaps you have a similar physical *hearth* such as this maiden? Perhaps yours is out of doors in a nearby park? Perhaps a beloved individual is your *hearth* and home? Wherever your *hearth* is, it is a space of connection, sharing, and exchange that sparks a sense of belonging, a space in which you can share tidings of great joy and sorrow, and know that you remain loved.

Hearth

Sing, Fire!
Muse of Transition,
shimmer the courage
of the labyrinth hearth within
     You,
Me,
     Us,
to stride the landscape
primeval,
whose invitation
     to tell it slant
prisms
     You,
Me,
     Us,
as prelude to the
        insistent tide
           of becoming.

Pausing at Our Thresholds

1. The Latin word for *hearth* is *focus*, meaning a *central, integral part of a home.* This Winter, what do you want to focus on? What tidings do you wish to share as a focus at your *hearth*?

2. What prisms your *hearth* during this time of year? How do the shades of the prism color your experiences? What colors are they? Wear something in those colors today.

3. Go to your *hearth-space.* Still your breathing. Share your tidings of the day.

Tidings

Pronunciation: /ˈtʌɪdɪŋ/ Inflections: plural tidings /ˈtaɪdɪŋz/
Function: Noun and Verb

Tidings debuts in Late Old English as tídung, a verb meaning *to happen, befall* plus the *-ing* suffix, leading to early Middle English *tiding*. It's derived from Old Norse *tíðendi* meaning *events, occurrences, the reports of these, news.* What's delightful is that early Middle English carried both forms, *tiding* and *tíðendi*, depending on whether one was sharing news in the south or north of England, respectively.

Tidings continues to signify *an announcement of an event or occurrence, a bit of news,* but it also once referred to *the flowing or rising of the tide.* Nowadays, this word tends to flow into our conversations only during the Winter season, in songs, cards, and carols as we gather to share what's happening in our lives.

Tidings. Announcements and reports of events often seem to ebb and flow on the tides of our days. *Tidings* carries a scent of expectation and breathlessness of a long-ago happening. *Have you heard the tidings?* We can imagine great-grand parents meeting up with friends in the street to wish each other *good tidings* or a town crier sharing momentous happenings, such as a declaration of peace between warring countries. In 1839, Thomas Carlyle wrote, "The tidings was world-old, or older." This sentence captures for me this sense of *tidings*—that which is as old as the undercurrents beneath our ocean surface.

Regardless of whether we are speaking of nineteenth century life or today, when *tidings* comes out to play, we have sharing; we have people coming together to discover the latest events, news or happenings that are *tiding* the currents in our personal friendships or in our wider communities. The Spinning Masterpiece on which we live shares with us the *tidings* of the seasons, as we ride the world-old course of her happenings into the time of stillness and rejuvenation that is Winter.

Tidings

In the early hours of the day,
Our Mother gently turns us
toward the Star that feeds us.

We are her winter blooms,
rotating our heads toward the play of light,
as our toes burrow into the loam of our stories.

This love light feeds us,
circulates in through our veins,
out through our arteries,
pulsing tidings of comfort and joy.

Such scarlet beauty quivers,
reveling in the edges of thresholds,
where we are swaddled tight
for one more turning.

Pausing at Our Thresholds

1. What are the *tidings* of comfort and joy that you wish to share this Winter?

2. What *tidings* do you fear during this season? How might resting within the thresholds in your life give you space to share? to heal?

3. Be still. What *tidings* are quivering in you at this moment? In the air that you are breathing? In the space you are occupying? What do they sound like? Remind you of? What might it feel like to touch them?

Be

Pronunciation: Brit. /biː/, U.S. /bi/   Function: Verb

Be, from the Old English *bēo, bēom*, was born into the Germanic family, descended from a plethora of Indo-European roots: Sanskrit *bhū*, Avestan *bū-*; Old Persian *bū-, biyā*; Gaulish *buet*; Early Irish *boí*; Old Church Slavonic *by-, bimĭ*; and classical Latin *fu* -, among others. It has relatives in: Old Saxon *bium, biun*; Old Frisian *bem, bim, ben, bin*; Old Dutch *bim, bin*; and Old High German *bim, bin*.

Be, which has been part of the human conversation for the past 6,000 years, tells us that we *have a place in the objective universe or realm of fact*, that we *exist independently of other beings in life*. That we *live*. It is our most complicated verb in English, the only one with eight different forms: *be, am, is, are, was, were, been,* and *being*. This complicated petite verb is a fitting tribute to the majestic diversity of the human experience of *being*.

Be, this simple syllable, has marked human existence *as existence* for millennia. In its travels across time and landscape, it has pulled together bits and pieces from at least three Indo-European roots to create the pattern, or paradigm, that we once learned in elementary school. Remember this?

To Be

I am/was	We are/were
You are/were	You are/were
S/He/It is/was	They are/ were

I *am*. You *are*. I *was*. You *were*. She *is*. They *were*. *Be, been, being* all come from one root, *bʰúHt*, meaning *to become, to grow*; while *am, are, art* and *is* come from **h₁ésmi*, and *h₁ésti*, meaning *I am, I exist*, and finally, *was* and *were* come from a third root, **h₂wes-* , meaning *to reside*. Our Eurasian ancestors, scattered across the horizon far and near, gathered around their Winter hearths to share the stories of their days, using these words to capture their experience of *becoming, existing,* and *residing*. It seems so fitting that our pattern of *be,* our word that states we *have a place in the objective universe,* draws from a diversity of roots, a complexity of human experience to capture that we *live,* together, then and there, here and now.

The following poem plays off a long-ago experience of having had to memorize the verb paradigm of 'to be' in Latin and the unexpected gifts and good tidings that came from that.

Be

Midday on a downtown sidewalk,
in a sparkling December breeze,
Ribbons of being rush
to   through
         here   and   there.
Our ribbons catch –
         Entwine and entangle
                  with the laughter of recognition.
         "Of course! We had freshman Latin together."
You nod, harrumphing in our teacher's voice:
         "Please state the principal parts of the verb 'to be.'"

And, once again,
         as if the world had not grown older,
the metallic taste of that command performance
         floods my senses:
         "I froze that day in class,
                  but you whispered the first Word to me."
Gratitude greets generosity once more,
         holds tenderly the reciprocal remembrance
of that awkward teenage gentleness.

Roses on our cheeks.
Rhythms of exchange.
Garlands in the wind
         chanting the ancient cadence of:

Sum, Esse, Fui, Futurus

Sum	I am
Esse	to be
Fui	I was/have been
Futurus	about to exist

one day, on the sidewalk,
    with you,
again.

Pausing at Our Thresholds

1. Where is your place of *being* in the objective universe at this moment?

2. On which sidewalks of life are you experiencing moments of living and *being* when you engage with an old friend or a stranger? Is the stranger yourself?

3. Rest for a moment. Let the tidings of life flow over you. Now, complete the following sentences:

I was …

I am …

I will be …

Holly

Pronunciation: 'hä-lE; plural hollies   Function: Noun

Holly's roots run through the Middle English *holin*, from the Old English *holen*; akin to Old High German *hulis*, Middle Irish *cuilenn*, with *holen* as cousin to Welsh *celyn*, Cornish *celin*, Breton *kelen*, Irish *cuillean*.

Holly or *hollin*, a now archaic form that still pops up in conversation in Scotland, hails from the *Aquifoliaceae family of trees and shrubs, with spiny-margined evergreen leaves and usually red berries.* Only the female holly shrub produces berries, requiring a male plant nearby for fertilization. *A plant often used for Christmas decorations.* When hanging mistletoe and holly, one must hang the mistletoe first—or risk ill luck during the Yuletide. In heraldry, holly symbolizes *truth.*

Holly, with its vibrant scarlet berries nestled in deep green leaves, bursts bright against the dusty greys and browns of the Winter landscape. The evergreen strength of *holly*, as well as its counterpart *ivy*, represents resiliency for enduring dramatic change. Because of this in-your-face living-despite-the-odds tenacity, *holly* has been accounted a plant of good omen since the earliest of times, protecting us from demons, house goblins and other troublesome creatures. For the Romans, *holly* represents Saturn, so they decorated with it for Saturnalia; for the Celts and Druids, *holly* represents fertility and eternal life, so it was worn in the hair and placed in the home for good luck and protection during Winter Solstice; for Christians, *holly* is whispered to have bloomed in the footprints of Jesus, its bright berries a gift of sacrificial love for Christmas; for Wiccans, the Holly King represents the face of the Sun God who rules the heavens from Mabon to Ostara. Within these and other traditions, *holly* welcomes us to joy and fellowship, brings us tidings of good luck and cheer. We gather it to celebrate our hearths, our horizons, and our holy moments of Winter within ourselves and with others.

Holly

Your Grandmother's basket is waiting,
as autumn slips away –
into the first twinklings
of frost and a canopy of crystal light.
It beckons, whispers:
Pick me up
Carry me into the fresh air
Fill me with sharp leaves
whose points tickle my sides
and whose red berries
hold the brilliance of the Sun.
Fill me
to honor Those
Who shimmer in the Life about you,
Who have filled their own baskets
      – and yours, too,
      many times –
to deck the halls
with boughs of holly.

–In gratitude to the traditional carol, "Deck the Halls" which has a Welsh melody from the sixteenth century. It is from a Winter carol called "Nos Galan" with lyrics by the Welsh bard Talhaiarn, who was a poet and architect by the name of John Jones (1810–1869). Thomas Oliphant, a Scottish musician, wrote the English lyrics around 1862.

Pausing at Our Thresholds

1. Who or what is the *holly* that brings you good cheer and joy in this season of celebration? How might you arrange your Winter days to spend more time with the *holly-bearers* in your life?

2. *Holly* is a symbol of truth in the language of heraldry. What tidings of truth are amongst the *holly* leaves and berries for you this season? Could you sketch out a coat of arms featuring your truths?

3. Take a deep breath. Look around you. Who or what is shimmering in the Life about you that has filled your basket many times? Take a moment to say thank you.

Ivy

Pronunciation: Brit. /ˈʌɪvi/, U.S. /ˈaɪvi/   Function: Noun

Ivy has grown from the Old High German *ebah*, which then wound its way into Old English *ífig*, and Middle English *ivi*, before becoming the word we use today.

    Ivy is a widely cultivated ornamental plant climbing or prostrate or sometimes a shrubby chiefly Eurasian vine (Hedera helix) of the ginseng family with evergreen leaves, small yellowish flowers, and black berries. The ancient Celts believed that *ivy*, along with its evergreen companions of holly and mistletoe, houses sylvan spirits that subdue our home goblins as the Winter winds howl about us.

    Ivy. The ancient Greeks tell a tale of a maiden who danced with such abandonment for Dionysus, the god of revelry, wine, and chaos, that she collapsed dead at his feet. The god, so touched by her passionate gift, offered one in return, placing her spirit into the plant that bears her name, *Ivy*, or that which embraces fully and tenaciously. Such tenacity is why *ivy* was considered a symbol of fidelity, wound into crowns, wreaths, or garlands. For the early Christians, it became a symbol of prosperity and charity, a reminder to reach out and embrace those in need. Together with holly, it was believed to protect homes from Christmas Eve, December 24th, until the decorations were taken down forty days later on Candlemas Eve, February 1st. In many Yuletide pagan traditions, the *Ivy* Queen is the perennial partner for the Holly King.

    Ivy, which can climb fifty feet up a wall or thrive as ground cover, is adaptable, meeting the needs of its environment. It flourishes with the music of sunlight, water, and soil, embracing all it encounters, whether that be in the high marks of Summer or in the cold depths of Winter. Such flourishing, particularly when combined with its partner holly, offers tidings of hope, manifested in green leaves lacing a gentle snow, and stories of steadfastness and determination.

Ivy

The chill of evening comes softly,
draped in indigo, violet, and rose.
We knit our winter stories with skeins of evergreen ivy,
stitching with a scent of cinnamon and
purling with a hint of pine.
Warm as scarves and mittens,
these stories cling to our bodies,
saturate skin and bone,
run through the currents of our marrow.

They burrow in for the season,
resting within us;
until,
leaping up into the dance of dawn,
they entangle
      ancestor with offspring,
           biped with quadruped,
      winged with earth-bound,
in the creaturely ways of our being.

Pausing at Our Thresholds

1. What do you wish to embrace with abandon during this season of good tidings? If you are already embracing it, are you clinging loosely enough for fresh air and sunshine to circulate and nurture? If you're not yet embracing it, what is preventing you from doing so? Can you name one thing that might move you into that relationship?

2. What *ivy* stories are saturating your skin and bone, running through the currents of your marrow? Is it time to prune or water? To let old stories fade or to tell them again? If to tell them again, think about sharing them in a new way: if you normally tell them orally, then write them down in a letter; if you normally tell them on Facebook, then pick up the phone; if you normally tell them quickly, then consider slowing down and writing or collaging them in a journal to share them with yourself or others in a fresh way.

3. *Be still.* Feel the *ivy* of your life embracing you with abandon. What's one action you might take to refresh the healthy vines in preparation for the surfacing of Spring?

Auld Lang Syne

Pronunciation: Brit. / ˌɔːld laŋ ˈsʌɪn/, / ˌəʊld laŋ ˈsʌɪn/, / ˌɔːld laŋ ˈzʌɪn/, / ˌəʊld laŋ ˈzʌɪn/, U.S. / ˌoʊl(d) ˌlæŋ ˈzaɪn/, / ˌɔl(d) ˌlæŋ ˈzaɪn/, / ˌɑl(d)ˌ læŋ ˈzaɪn/, Scottish/ ˌɔld ˌlang ˈsaɪn/

Function: Adjective + Adverb to form a Noun Phrase

Auld Lang Syne sings itself to us from Scottish Gaelic in several forms: *ald lang syne, old long syne, auld lang syne,* and *old lang syne.* It's formed by joining the adjective *auld* with the adverb *langsyne,* meaning *old long since,* or translated as *times long ago.*

In 1796, the Scottish poet, Robert Burns, heard an elderly man sing an ancient folk song about cherishing friendship. Burns recognized the song as a treasure to be preserved. So, he wrote down the lyrics and sent them to the Scots Musical Museum. The elderly singer's musical generosity and Burn's quick thinking have given us the song we now sing to honor friendship, shared memories, and the fading of the old year, as the clock strikes midnight on New Year's Eve.

Auld Lang Syne. It is late at night on the Midwinter's watch. We catch our breath when someone begins to sing. We stumble over the lyrics. Maybe because we usually only sing it once a year? Maybe because it's a strange mix of familiar and unfamiliar words in a strange order? Maybe simply because the Earth and the Sun together bring us tidings of great joy—but poignant joy—as the old year is set free and the new one is welcomed? Regardless, this ancient phrase taps into the depths of the human primeval as we sing together:

> *Should auld acquaintance be forgot,*
> *and never brought to mind?*
> *Should auld acquaintance be forgot,*
> *and auld lang syne?*

> *For auld lang syne, my jo,*
> *for auld lang syne,*
> *we'll tak' a cup o' kindness yet,*
> *for auld lang syne.*

The following poem invites us to pause in the poignancy of feeling and story that this olden tune ignites within us. It is an invitation to welcome the tidings of a new year even as we grieve the passing of the old one—or vice versa. For whatever is the musical magic of this gift from a generous bard and a world class poet, it marks our yearly threshold when we contemplate the bitter sweetness of time passing.

Auld Lang Syne

It is a cold night.
Together,
      let us keep the Winter Watch.
Put the kettle on.
Pull the chairs close to the fire.
Pour out stories
      from the wilderness of memory.

Let us kindle the telling,
lasso the tale,
laugh, rest, and
listen to the yearning
of *auld lang syne*,
whispering in the pines.

We'll take that cup of kindness yet,
and quietly,
oh, so quietly,
rejoice
in the tenderness
that life begets.

Pausing at Our Thresholds

1. What is the cup of kindness you wish to share and receive this Winter?

2. What quiet tenderness do you wish to bestow or accept this Winter?

3. Pour a cup of tea or coffee, or a glass of water or wine. What tidings from *auld lang syne*, of *times long ago*, do you wish to toast, cherish or relinquish in the coming year? Toast them. Reckon with them.

Dance

Pronunciation: Brit. /dɑːns/, /dans/, U.S. /dæns/
Function: Noun and Verb

Dance springs from the Old French verb *dancer*, twirling with partners such as Provençal *dansar*, Spanish *danzar*, Portuguese *dançar*, *dansar*, and Italian *danzare*. It is generally believed that the Old French *dancer* can be traced to the Old High German *dansôn*, meaning *to draw, to stretch out, from which is supposed to have arisen the sense 'to form a file or chain in dancing.'* The Gothic cousin of *pinsan* meant to *draw towards one.*

    Dance is the human body in motion, *leaping, skipping, hopping, or gliding with measured steps and rhythmical movements of the body, usually to the accompaniment of music, either by oneself, or with a partner or in a set.*

    Dance. As a verb, it is intransitive, meaning that it doesn't take a direct object (remember *that* idea from fifth grade English class?); nothing or no one receives the action, grammatically. But we know better than that, experientially. For when we dance, we receive the actions of our bodies in motion as do our dance partners, and any and all who may be enjoying the music with us. This is why the Sugar Plum Fairy in Tchaikovsky's *Nutcracker* leaps and spins to celebrate with Clara and the Prince; why the Mummers *dance* in the guise of the King Stag during Yuletide; and why the Ghost of Christmas Past whisks Ebenezer Scrooge back to a holiday *dance* of his youth with the cheerful and light-footed Mr. and Mrs. Fezziwig in Dickens' *A Christmas Carol.* All of these dances—the 19th century ballet, the ancient folk traditional, and the Victorian *Sir Roger de Coverley*,— remind us that we share tidings through our bodies, just as we do our words. The following poem grew from a deep enchantment performed late on a Winter's night, when I witnessed several trees *dance* in a captivating harmony, in the ballroom that was my front lawn.

Dance

Moonlight spotlights the shimmering lawn.
The mischievous breeze breathes life,
    into the dancers.

Center Stage – Metamorphosis I
The magic dust of midwinter sprinkles
the spindly legs and arms of the Crepe Myrtle,
            freeing Tchaikovsky's shadowy ballerinas to bow
and sway to the Sugar Plum Fairy,
        who dips slightly,
            in time with her breezy partner.

Stage Left – Metamorphosis II
The magic dust of midwinter sprinkles
the sturdy arms and legs of the Oak,
        releasing the proud stag,
            whose antler crown bows and sways
            in rhythm with the Mummer's tune.

Stage Right – Metamorphosis III
The magic dust of midwinter sprinkles
the still-leafy arms and legs of the towering Sycamore,
        vivifying the Fezziwigs to bow and sway,
                hoop skirts, pantaloons,
            and feathered top hats
in step with the fiddler,

as the deep blue velvet of the dance
        fades into the genesis,
            of the rising of the sun
                and the running of the deer.

—In gratitude to the British Christmas carol, "The Holly and the Ivy," which can be traced back to the nineteenth century, even though it contains much older, medieval references. The most popular contemporary version was documented by the English folk song collector Cecil Sharp in 1909 in Chipping Campden, Gloucestershire, England. Sharp's informant was a woman called Mary Clayton.

Pausing at Our Thresholds

1. What tidings are making you tap your toe or bow and sway in this season?

2. What magic are you experiencing in the *dance* of your body this season?

3. Walk outside. Bow to the trees in gratitude for their daily *dance* by which they clean our air and replenish our oxygen. Think about accepting their invitation to *dance* with them at the rising of the sun. How might you thank them for their present and their presence?

Joy

The theme of *Joy* shoots from the wellspring of Latin's *gaudium*, meaning *gladness*, which then traveled to France, where in Old French it meant *jewel*. And what a lustrous *jewel* it is in our lives: *joy*. As we settle in for the reckoning of Winter, for its sharp winds and cutting ice, our *joys* are often simple ones: the burst of warm air that hugs us when we walk into our homes, the softness of the worn cotton of a favorite pair of mittens, or the glistening of the eyes of our Beloveds when we greet each other—on the streets, in our offices, at our homes, over a Zoom call. We have a special word that has emerged in the last couple decades that captures this feeling of relationships generating joy: *symhedonia*, or the *joy we experience when we celebrate the gifts and success of each other, a joy that manifests the bonds of sympathy amongst us*. When we allow ourselves to nestle into such a sympathetic joy, to still ourselves so as to be open to the tidings of others, we expand our horizons to discover ourselves bound in the cosmic circle of humans being together.

Enjoy the words and poems that anchor the meditations rooted in the theme of *Joy*:

Joy, Sing, Magi, Wassail, Merriment, Ornament, and *Twinkle*.

Joy

Pronunciation: Brit. /dʒɔɪ/, U.S. /dʒɔɪ/   Function: Noun

Joy springs forth from the well of Latin *gaudium*, meaning *gladness, delight*, which then flows into Old French *joie, joye*, meaning *jewel*, into Middle English, as well as into Provençal *joia*, Spanish *joya*, Portuguese *joia*, and Italian *gioja*.

 Joy, a simple syllable, whether in English, French or Portuguese, has always carried with it a meaning of *vivid emotion of pleasure arising from a sense of well-being or satisfaction; the feeling or state of being highly pleased; exultation of spirit; gladness*. In other words, *joy* is a feeling that infuses our-selves and others with *delight*. That is a precious gift for all of us as the days grow shorter, the nights grow longer, and the cold grows deeper.

 Joy, like a virus, is contagious. We radiate with it, as it seeps out, pours out, reaches out to connect with those near to us. I recently asked my husband what's the first thing he thinks of when he hears the word *joy*. He replied immediately, "Music!" Lyrics and melodies, pianos and percussion, winds and strings, swirl together and take us with them. Carlos Santana, marvelous musician that he is, also reminds us that, "if you carry *joy* in your heart, you can heal any moment." Indeed! And how we need that healing of *joy* at this moment in time. For me, such healing *joy* often comes from unexpected invitations. I originally drafted the poem below as a response to such an invitation, from an esteemed mentor, to participate in an indige-nous language revitalization project. The tribal elders and youths, along with the scholars, are breathing fresh life and healing into the melodies and stories of a nearly lost Native American language. Together they are listen-ing deeply to the past so as to carry the *joy* of the sounds and words of this language into the future. I find their delight and satisfaction in this work to be contagious. My husband finds an exultation of spirit in music to be con-tagious. Perhaps a source of *joy* for you in the bleak midwinter is simply a hot cup of coffee and a few minutes of quiet snatched from the bustle of the season, or a quick visit with an old friend you run into on the sidewalk as the cold wind blows about you? Perhaps it is a feeling of deep satisfaction from having survived a particularly challenging experience or relationship? Perhaps it is a gladness of a difficult task being completed with dignity? Sometimes, it is just a deep breath, or the hoot of an owl at dusk, or the snow falling gently that throws open the windows of our being, allowing the contagion of *joy* to capture us in a flash of symhedonia.

Joy

The invitation has set my
heart-mind aflutter,
set me adrift,
guiding my eyes,
my tongue
my fingers,
through a new moment of sound,
taking shape into story.

The letters and lift of the past
sieve the blood inside me,
until I am buoyed
with the ancient joy
of future listening.

Pausing at Our Thresholds

1. What invitations are setting your heart-mind aflutter with *joy* during this time of the year?

2. What invitations might you issue or music might you discover this Winter to create *the vivid emotion of pleasure arising from a sense of well-being or satisfaction*?

3. Stop. Look around. Is there a smell, taste, sound, view or touch that brings *joy* to you at this very moment? If so, experience your gratitude for it; if not, what can you change in the moment to lead you to *an exultation of spirit or symhedonia*?

Sing

Pronunciation: 'si[ng]   Function: Verb

Sing has ridden the winds of the Old English *singan*, cousin to Old High German and Old Saxon *singan*, Old Frisian *sionga*, Middle Dutch *singen*, Old Norse *syngva* and Gothic *siggwan*, for nearly two thousand years. It's possibly related to the Greek *omphE*, meaning *voice of the gods or the oracle*. Doesn't that seem fitting that the voice of the gods should be shared in song?

Sing not only sparks melody and rhythm in our world when *we produce musical tones by means of the voice, with musical inflections and modulations*; it also *celebrates something in verse, poetry to create in or through words a feeling or sense of song*, whether that be light or heavy, pensive or frivolous. We often *sing to bring or accompany to a place or state by singing*, such as when we *sing* a child to sleep with a lullaby. When we *sing*, we experience the consequences, physical and emotional, of our songs, resonating not only within us but within others as well.

Sing! Of stillness and joy that birth our world each year, as the Earth turns on its axis, and once more, the days grow longer after the measure of the long night. In much of classical poetry, the Muse *sings* the tale alive, her breath a chain reaction of trembling into a point and counterpoint of plot and character. This is the tradition I drew from for the opening of the poem "Hearth" which commands, "*Sing*, Fire!" The Muse stands as the goddess-oracle voice of genesis, exploding into Big Bangs while flying with Prometheus and Raven as they steal the Sun. Her *singing* generates creativity, an ordering of our chaos into something new, whether that's a new poem, a new year, or a new world.

The following poem returns to an ancient story, a story of a god *singing* a world into existence in seven days, recognizing its goodness, and then resting. A day-by-day Genesis of

- ♥ Day1: Light,

- ♥ Day 2: Sky,

- ♥ Day 3: Land,

- ♥ Day 4: Cosmos,

- ♥ Day 5: Creatures of Sea and Air,

- ♥ Day 6: Creatures of the Land, and

- ♥ Day 7: Rest.

A rather intense To Do List. *Singing* swells from the breath, from a deep *h*-sound, that *hah* that we pull up and out from the caves of our lungs, swelling with the bravery of our hearts. As I wrote this poem, I kept finding myself breathing out that deep *hah* and searching for verbs that started with this sound, verbs that move us to creation. I unearthed a couple of ones new to me and perhaps new to you as well. *Hightle* and *high-mettle* are classified as obsolete in contemporary English, but they aren't any longer in my world. I think they are marvelous and worthy of a fresh breath. *Hightle* means to *adorn or ornament something*; whereas *high-mettle* means to *make courageous, spirited or vitalized*—perhaps, and in particular—through the harmonious joy of song.

Sing!

Sing a Song of the Seven Days
     with the counterpoint of night
to ease the way.

Hold the measure to fathom the firmament of the heavens
     from the briny depths of dominion.

Harmonize the spheres of land and sea
     with the treble clefs of plants and trees.

Herald the celestial symphony of sun and moon and stars.

Hightle the wind with feathered majesty
     and the waters with gleaming scales.

High-mettle the two and four legged creatures
     in a chorus of courage rampant.

Hover in the blaze of stillness,
     of notes blended into beauty,

Then rest,
Oh, gods of creation,
Rest.

Pausing at Our Thresholds

1. As we measure the firmaments of our lives, in the depths of Winter darkness, what do you wish to *sing* into creative joy?

2. What areas of your life might you hightle? Where do you or a loved one need to be high-mettled?

3. Look up from this page. What songs of creative joy are you living in this moment? *Sing* those songs in any way that feels appropriate for you.

Magi

Pronunciation. Singular magus Brit. /ˈmeɪɡəs/,U.S. /ˈmeɪɡəs/; Plural magi, Brit. /ˈmeɪdʒʌɪ/, U.S. /ˈmeɪˌdʒaɪ/, /ˈmæˌdʒaɪ/
Function: Noun

Magi is a borrowed word from classical Latin, its etymon *magus*, singular, with *magi* as the plural. Its family includes the ancient Greek μάγος, *mágos*, magician, and the Old Persian *maguš*.

Magi, for those Romans who spoke classical Latin, *denoted a member of the Persian priestly class, and, more broadly, priests or wise men of other nations.* It's chiefly spelt with an initial capital *M*, when it designates the three *Magi*, or the 'wise men' or astronomers who came from the East, bearing gifts to the infant Jesus in the Christian Gospel of Matthew 2:1–12. These are the same gift-bearers who outsmarted the tyrant, King Herod, who had wanted a report from them after they had found the infant. *The Magi.*

Magi are generous wisdom figures who are steadfast, even when it is inconvenient and dangerous. If we are lucky, if we are open, if we are even a slight bit curious, we can spot the *magi* walking with us and among us each day. The image we have of three kings in rich robes, riding camels into the night, bearing rare gifts, too often blinds us to the *magi* presence in our work-a-day lives. Maybe it's the person in the cubicle next to yours, who reads a room quickly enough to save you from yourself, that is a magus. Maybe it's the family member who sits quietly at the holiday gathering, soaking in the ebb and flow of the relationships, that is a *magus*. Maybe it's the disabled veteran, who volunteers to teach your dyslexic child to read after school, that is the *magus*. Regardless of where and who, the *magi* have a sense of timing, of knowing what to give when, to whom, even if they, themselves, don't own a warm coat, have a home, or eat a regular hot meal.

The following poem tells the story of a *Magi* visit to a holiday meal provided for the homeless in San Antonio, Texas. The three wise men looked just like everyone else in the food line that day until...

Until they gifted everyone in the hall with such beauty that we looked at each other, startled by the recognition that this was a moment when we would say, years later, "Yes, I was there, in that hall, that day, listening with joy, with symhedonia."

Magi

In through the East door,
damp from drizzle,
the three men walk warily to piles of
blankets, coats, and socks,
take up plastic bags, fill them with the promised warmth,
place them gently next to the metal chairs lining
the long dining table.

Warming, they approach the food counter,
say *hello*, accept heaping plates.
Others arrive, join them at their table.
Conversation hums over turkey,
cranberry sauce, and pecan pie.

Satisfied, in unison, The Trio rises
and surprises us,
>surprises us by
>>breaking into song!

A prelude of scat
wakes the room,
>sets the rhythm,
>>releases joy,

for a crooning of an *a capella* memoir
>of the power of gold,
>the blessings of frankincense,
>the sacrifice of myrrh,

and other acts of reckless generosity
>saturated in grace.

Joy incarnate! Have you ever experienced it?

Notes skitter across the tables,
    along the walls, and
        around the floorboards.

The Magi   bring   it   HOME!

Now everyone is on their feet,
the applause heard down the street,
a celebration of thanks complete –
as sacramental effervescence matures us
in the amniotic fluid of bounty.

We are breathless. We are alive – together
in that magic flash of communion.

The Magi smile,
laugh in rich tones,
    accept our thanks for their giving.

After a denouement of smiles and handshakes,
they shoulder their bags,
    as easily as their talent,
        and slip out the West door
        into the winter night.

Pausing at Our Thresholds

1. Who are *The Magi* who bring joy to you?

2. For you, what is the relationship between joy and serving others?

3. Think for a moment. Do the *Magi* of your life know how much you appreciate them? If not, let them know during this season of the long nights. Write them a note or give them a call to tell them.

Wassail

Pronunciation: Brit. /ˈwɒseɪl/; U.S. /ˈwɑsəl/
Function: Noun and Verb

Wassail brings good tidings to us from Old Norse *ves heill* which corresponds with the Old English *wes hál*, meaning to *be in good health* or *be fortunate*, and with the Middle English *wæs hæil*.

Wassail as an *ordinary salutation, such as hail or farewell*, occurs in Old English as *hál wes þú* (singular), as *wesað hále* (plural), and in Old Norse plural as *verið heilir*. *Wassail* is also a traditional *salutation used when presenting a cup of wine to a guest, or drinking the health of a person, with the courteous reply being drinc hail*, meaning *drink good health* or *good luck*. It is a toast to friendship with friend and foe, alike. *Wassail* is larger and more gracious than enmity.

Wassail, in traditional English folk custom, can be used as both a greeting and a farewell, like *Aloha* in Hawaii or *Hello* in Hungary. As a toast, *wassail*, sealed pacts of friendship between friends and foes at any time of the year. Such toasting was not limited just to blessings for fellow humans, but for all of creation. On Christmas Eve (December 24th) or on Twelfth Night (January 6th), fruit trees, like apple, plum and pear, as well as oxen and other livestock were also honored with a warm spiced ale, sometimes called *lamb's wool*, made with hot apples bubbling and hissing within, and with *wassail cakes*. In 1648, Robert Herrick celebrated this in *Hesperides*, saying, "Wassaile the Trees, that they may beare You many a Plum, and many a Peare"; while in 1686, John Aubrey in *Remaines Gentilisme & Judaisme*, recalled that "at Twelve-tyde at night they use in the Countrey to wassaile their Oxen and to have Wassaile-Cakes made." Nearly 200 years later, the blessings still flowed as the custom, in the cider districts of Sussex, was to *worsle* or *wassail* the apple trees.

This tradition of *ves heill* is not the only phrase that the Vikings shared with their conquered English brethren. They also brought with them words we still use each and every day like *guest*, *wind*, and *awe*. Words that sparkle during the *Yuletide*—another offering from Old Norse.

The following poem is crafted around such borrowings, with each word printed in **bold** being from Old Norse while only those few printed in *italics* being from Old English. Perhaps we might call this a 'Norse-glish' poem?

Wassail

Tidings run,
riven *with* **wassail,**
kindling *the* **saga** *of* Yule.

Hail *the* **bands** *of* **fellowship:**
knots *in the* **bark** *of the apple, plum, and pear* –
bellows *of* **reindeer basking** *in the* **fog.**
Guests *of* **awe, skirted** *and* **gloved,**
freckled *with* **happiness.**

Amongst the **gusts,**
they skate *beyond the* **glittering windows,**
calling *a* **jolly ado** *to the* **gosslings,**
whose **wings birth** *the* **winds,**
as **they take**
        to a **bleak** *midwinter* **sky.**

Pausing at Our Thresholds

1. What gifts do you want to *wassail* during these days of a bleak midwinter sky?

2. What tidings, riven with *wassail*, do you hope for your own saga in the coming year?

3. Pause. Consider your current relationships. Is there an enemy or foe to whom you are ready to *wassail, wish joy and good health*? If so, perhaps setting down that burden might bring joy in this season of glittering windows and bands of fellowship. Write or sketch what such an encounter might look like, taste like, and/or sound like.

Merriment

Pronunciation: Brit. /ˈmɛrɪm(ə)nt/, U.S. /ˈmɛrɪm(ə)nt/
Function: Noun

Merriment is dually derived from the etymons of *merry*, an adjective, + *-ment*, a suffix that transforms that adjective into a noun. The glamour of grammar right in this word—magic! The history of the meaning of *merry* also has a two-part, dual nature. Part one is its grounding in Old English *myrge*, which means *pleasing, agreeable, pleasant, sweet, exciting feelings of enjoyment and gladness*; whereas part two is grounded in Proto-Germanic **murgijaz*, which probably originally meant something that was *pleasantly and melodiously and short-lasting*. Time is of, and in, the essence for *merriment*.

Merriment's history reminds us that "time is the fire in which we burn" to quote the poet Delmore Schwartz. Our time to make *merry*, to *participate in amusing and enjoyable activities; fun and gaiety; exuberant enjoyment*, is brief. An obsolete meaning of *merriment* is that of a *festivity*. So, the party, itself. Like *hittle* and *high-mettle*, perhaps it's time to rejuvenate this meaning of *merriment*, as we experience the pleasant and melodious exuberant joys of warmth and gathering, during these long nights.

Merriment. It's an old-fashioned word. We use it rarely nowadays. *Merry* partnering with *Christmas* continues to be a popular greeting and sentiment. But *merriment*? That takes us back to previous eras. Eras of open fields lying quiet under night skies free of light pollution. Eras before digital devices buzzed with social media notifications demanding our immediate attention. We don't have to give them our immediate attention, though, do we? If we don't, would that leave us some *short-lasting time for exciting feelings of enjoyment and gladness*, that we might dive into? A *festivity* that we might share to bring ourselves and others joy? In other words, might we have a brief moment of *exuberant joy*, of *merriment*? Maybe we can even incorporate those ting tang chimes of notifications into our *merriment*. Want to risk it with me? We don't have to risk it just for ourselves, either. Like wassailing involving trees and oxen in earlier times, *merriment* also has a history involving hounds and birds and organs and all other sorts of fun.

In "Sir Gawain & the Green Knight" (c1390) both men and hounds are said to be *merry*:

> Mony watz þe [m] yry mouthe of men & of houndez/
> Many was the *merry* mouth of men and hounds.

In Thomas Malory's *Morte D'Arthur* (1470), the blithe country is filled with merry birds:

> They trotted on…over a blythe contray full of many myrry byrdis.
> They trotted on … over a blithe country full of many merry birds.

In C.J. Sharp's collection of English Folk Carols (1911), we sing in "The Holly and the Ivy" (1797) of the merry organ:

> The rising of the sun And the running of the deer,
> The playing of the merry organ,
> Sweet singing in the choir.

The following poem invites us to venture outside to join the stars enjoying their nightly festivities, to remember a sense of *merriment* that may be lying dormant in our own fields.

Merriment

A kinetic caress,
the Merriment of Stardust,
        lights gently on the faces
           of the children,
in the field.
They hum with anticipation,
pointing excitedly at

          the Dancing Tail of the Compass Rose:

ancient Lodestar for the wintry adventures
of kings, shepherds, and angelic hosts,
who sing of Wonderment,
        under the sparkling sequins that
          dapple the Ball Gown of Night.

Pausing at Our Thresholds

1. What ignites *merriment* within you? If the answer is nothing, what small change might you make to set it free within you?

2. *Merriment* is generally a shared experience. How might you offer a bit of *festivity* for someone you love or someone whom you know to be lonely? It doesn't have to be a complicated expression of *exuberant joy*, just authentic and heart-felt. Share a small treat like a favorite song, poem, a piece of chocolate, or an orange.

3. Walk around a bit. It can be either inside or outside. What ingredients for *merriment* are surrounding you at this very moment, just waiting for you to ignite them? A work colleague? A family member? An old friend? Vacation pictures? Old shoes? A favorite chair? Dance partners all. Perhaps begin by asking, "Do you remember when we...took that picture...found that chair...bought those shoes?" Add a little music. Maybe some bubbles or silly string or a whoopee cushion...and before you know it...*Merriment!*

Ornament

Pronunciation: Brit. /ˈɔːnəm(ə)nt/, U.S. /ˈɔrnəm(ə)nt/
Function: Noun

Ornament is partly a borrowing from French, partly a borrowing from Latin, with the following etymons: Anglo-Norman French *hournement, ornament, ornement, meaning to adorn, decorate, embellish*; Latin *ōrnāmentum*, meaning *equipment, trapping, circumstance conferring honour.* It has cousins in Old Occitan *ornamenta* (late 13th cent.), Spanish *ornamento* (1251), Catalan *ornament* (c1272), Italian *ornamento* (end of the 13th cent.), Portuguese *ornamento* (1337), and also Middle High German *ornament*, meaning *robes of office, ceremonial dress.*

 Ornament for us today tends to mean, *something used to adorn, beautify, or embellish, or that naturally does this; a decoration, embellishment.* We may embellish ourselves with decorations such as jewelry, or our homes with a treasure created by a child, or our work places with a recognition of our dedication. These pieces of beauty often reveal to us a bit of truth about what we value and cherish.

 Ornament. Is it surprising that it comes from a combination of borrowings and not a single source? It seems right to me. *Ornaments,* whether personal, in our homes, or in our holiday decorations are often eclectic, collected over time and landscapes traversed—by ourselves, our ancestors, our children, or other loved ones—leaving us with adornments of our being.

 There is a sense of connectedness when we speak of *ornaments,* these trappings of beauty, of honour, and of ceremony. They reference a special moment or event for us. They take us outside of ourselves, beautiful tentacles tethering us to touchstones of memories, both felt and thought.

 This creates a sense of inheritance when we think about *ornaments,* especially during this season of Winter Solstice. We inherit the beauty of the Sun tilting on its axis; we inherit the nose, mouth, smile or laughter of our mothers, grandfathers or long lost cousins; we inherit a seasonal decoration that has been in the family for generations. This inheritance sometimes imbues these *ornaments* with a heaviness, a poignancy that lightly holds loss and gift, grief and joy, simultaneously within our hearts and homes. The following poem attempts to tap into these senses of *ornaments*, of our traditions and patterns that have been handed down over generations in our particular families, or over eons in terms of our Sun and our beloved home of Earth, for our human family.

Ornament

The ornaments of this season
remind me of the reason,
we tie the ribbons and bows.

Tie the ribbons and bows!
    As the ground sighs
under its blanket of snow,
        we tinsel and garland the trees.

Tinsel and garland the trees!
    For the sun stands still
for the year to be,
        we welcome the return of the light.

Welcome the return of the light!
    For all that is good and right,
        we wander in its mystery bright,

weathering in the peace
    of our hightled nights.

Pausing at Our Thresholds

1. With what do you adorn the hightled nights of Winter? Are these *ornaments* an inheritance or an innovation of your own?

2. How do you adorn, beautify, or embellish yourself during this time of year?

3. Pick up an *ornament* from your life. Touch it, hold it for a minute or so. Bathe in the memories associated with it, reminding you why you cherish it. If it needs dusting, do it. If it needs repair, fix it. If it's time to hand it over to the next generation as their inheritance, let it go.

Twinkle

Pronunciation :/ˈtwɪŋk(ə)l/   Function: Noun and Verb

Twinkle hales from Old English stock, from the verb *twinclian* or **twin-can* with *twink* as a verb stem plus the *-le* suffix.

Twinkle has had a variety of meanings, some which we recognize today and others that have slipped into history. Some we recognize are *to shine with rapidly intermittent light; to emit tremulous radiance; to sparkle; to glitter; to glimmer; to flicker.* Others, such as *intermittent—to communicate a signal, or as a dance, to perform the twinkle step,* we might not be familiar with...but our imaginations can take us back to moments when we *twinkled* a signal that we were ready to hit the dance floor, sparkling, as our feet flickered with the celebration of being alive.

Twinkle. Geoffrey Chaucer, in the Prologue of his road trip adventure, *The Canterbury Tales*, introduces us to the Friar, saying,

> Hise eyen twinkled...As doon the sterres in the frosty nyght
>
> His eyes twinkled...as do the stars in the frosty night (c. 1387–1395).

Eyes that *twinkle*, like the Friar's, shine with generosity mixed with a wee bit of mischief on a frosty night. Four hundred years later, those same mischievous inviting eyes pop up in another description of a generous soul on a frosty night, Saint Nicholas. Clement C. Moore writes in his famous poem, "A Visit from St. Nicholas" ("'Twas the Night Before Christmas"),

> His eyes—how they twinkled! his dimples, how merry!
>
> His cheeks were like roses, his nose like a cherry!

This sense of joy, generosity, and invitation communicates a signal indeed when our eyes—or our feet—*twinkle.* When we discover *"in a twinkling,"* like the narrator of Moore's poem does when he hears the prancing and pawing of the reindeer on the roof, that we are members one of another. We are members in a shared dance in which we, "[C]hassèe to the left, two steps forward, two steps back, *twinkle* each way," as we did the *twinkle* step in the 1920s.

These dancing eyes and feet reveal us as portals of stardust through which we shine, inviting others into joy with us, into symhedonia. This last poem moves us into the joy of a day well-spent, into the gloaming or *glowing* hours as twilight welcomes us into respite.

Twinkle

There is that moment
when the sun slides
                Over the horizon
                    like a silk gown off
Once-young shoulders,

And the light tinges
purple and orange
the frosted glass
in the window pane,

And weariness ebbs from
feet, fingers, and face
in a contented sigh.

Rest fills this gloaming,
        anticipating
                the twinklings of twilight.

Pausing at Our Thresholds

1. What have you discovered in a *twinkling* that has brought joy to your life?

2. What *twinkle* steps might you dance this Winter to share tidings of joy with those on your horizons?

3. Stand up. Put on a favorite bit of music. Grab a partner and "[c]hassèe to the left, two steps forward, two steps back, [and] *twinkle* each way," allowing your body to generate joy. How does it feel?

Hopes for The Becoming

Love plays the long game in the dialectic of our becoming. My hope is that the words and stories highlighted in this collection have been worthy Winter companions, loving companions, in the dialectic of your own becoming.

Our Winters may last for several years or may last only for a few moments. We never quite know. However, regardless of the amount of time, we know that it is our actual acceptance of Winter's invitation, to journey over its threshold, that lets us embark on a season of growth. If we are lucky, Winter, with its starkness made visible, prunes us of thoughts that wither and habits that erode our joy, thereby freeing us from the repetition of patterns that undermine our sense of symmetry and well-being. Winter, with its deep ember nights, ornamented with bright holly, ivy, and mistletoe, tenders us a horizon from which we might imagine the dance of good tidings and believe in the magi who walk amongst us each day. It proffers stillness in which we can listen at our hearths, calm our yearnings, and sing the merriment of our beings, even as we wassail the snow-covered trees with whispers of *auld lang syne.*

Winter can steal upon us in a twinkling or bowl us over in an avalanche. We may never quite know how or when Janus may extend his hands to us and pull us on to that threshold. No matter. We know that we are here to play the long game, and will do so, crossing worthily into the roundedness of our own becoming.

Acknowledgements

Thank you to Cyra Dumitru and Andrea Ptak of River Lily Press, for their editorial and design gifts, as well as their support for and confidence in this project. The seeds of *Horizons of Joy* were first planted and tended over fifteen years ago, in a conversation with Rey Gustamente about the relationship between the seasons and contemplation. Rey and I met, more than once at the W.D. Deli on Broadway in San Antonio, to discuss this project, enjoy good food, and explore our latest answers for the urgent questions of our world. It was a gift that Wayne D. Beers and Michael Bobo, the proprietors, didn't kick us out after being there for so many hours, or make us start washing dishes to pay our rent. When COVID-19 gripped our world, W.D. Deli still provided good food curbside, and Rey steadfastly continued to support this project, for which I am so grateful. Sr. Elizabeth Hatzenbuehler graciously read a first draft and responded by painting the stunning watercolor that inspired *Horizons'* cover art. What an act of spontaneous munificence for which I am so thankful. I am also grateful to Carol Coffee Reposa, Eddie Vega, Julia Walsh, FSPA, and Nicki Prevou, who generously took time away from their own writing, to read and comment on *Horizons'* manuscript, with insight and kindness. Thank you to the Soul's Journey Poetry Circle, at the Ecumenical Center for Education, Counseling, and Health of San Antonio, which has watered and fertilized several poems in this project, with patience and wisdom. Finally, thank you to my family for their encouragement, love, and good humor as I completed this endeavor during some of the darkest days of the global COVID-19 pandemic. May we never experience that particular winter ever again.

CPSIA information can be obtained
at www.ICGtesting.com
Printed in the USA
LVHW071325181021
700759LV00018B/133